PRAISE FOR *BLACK, WHITE, COLORED*

"Histories of Black freedom movements foreground the importance of intergenerational knowledge to build new worlds. *Black, White, Colored* offers the opportunity to not only learn about the impact of cultivating knowledge on the author's family history but also its impact on the writing process."

—Dr. Soyica Diggs Colbert, PhD, Interim Provost and Idol Family Professor, Georgetown University

"We must honor history. I also believe we should embrace the uncomfortable in the past in order to move forward in the present and the future. Lauretta Malloy Noble and LeeAnét Noble, mother and daughter, and beneficiaries of an extraordinary family, do both brilliantly in their essential read."

—Gayle Jessup White, author of *Reclamation: Sally Hemings, Thomas Jefferson, and a Descendant's Search for Her Family's Lasting Legacy*

THE HIDDEN STORY OF AN INSURRECTION, A FAMILY, A SOUTHERN TOWN, AND IDENTITY IN AMERICA

AMISTAD
An Imprint of HarperCollins*Publishers*

BLACK, WHITE, COLORED

**LAURETTA MALLOY NOBLE
AND LEEANÉT NOBLE**

Without limiting the exclusive rights of any author, contributor or the publisher of this publication, any unauthorized use of this publication to train generative artificial intelligence (AI) technologies is expressly prohibited. HarperCollins also exercise their rights under Article 4(3) of the Digital Single Market Directive 2019/790 and expressly reserve this publication from the text and data mining exception.

BLACK, WHITE, COLORED. Copyright © 2025 by Lauretta Malloy Noble and LeeAnét Noble. All rights reserved. Printed in the United States of America. No part of this book may be used or reproduced in any manner whatsoever without written permission except in the case of brief quotations embodied in critical articles and reviews. For information, address HarperCollins Publishers, 195 Broadway, New York, NY 10007. In Europe, HarperCollins Publishers, Macken House, 39/40 Mayor Street Upper, Dublin 1, D01 C9W8, Ireland.

HarperCollins books may be purchased for educational, business, or sales promotional use. For information, please email the Special Markets Department at SPsales@harpercollins.com.

harpercollins.com

FIRST EDITION

Designed by Elina Cohen
Unless otherwise noted, photographs are provided by the authors.

Library of Congress Cataloging-in-Publication Data has been applied for.

ISBN 978-0-06-335222-3

25 26 27 28 29 LBC 5 4 3 2 1

To the ancestors and elders who had a collective vision of community, education, family, and economic growth, and created a stable place of respite in Laurinburg, North Carolina, enabling Black children to soar while the world was spinning

"When you know your name, you should hang on to it, for unless it is noted down and remembered, it will die when you do."

—Toni Morrison, *Song of Solomon*

Contents

Family Trees — xi

Introduction — xv

1. **Africans, Scots, and Americans** — *1*
2. **1865** — *17*
3. **Grandfather William** — *33*
4. **People and Places** — *47*
5. **A Backyard War** — *63*
6. **Post-Insurrection** — *77*
7. **Another New Beginning** — *93*
8. **Southern Tea** — *109*
9. **Coming of Age** — *123*
10. **Country to Town** — *141*
11. **Going Back to Move Forward** — *157*

Postscript: The Spirit Prevails — 173

Acknowledgments — 189

Notes — 197

William & Minnie and William & Annie

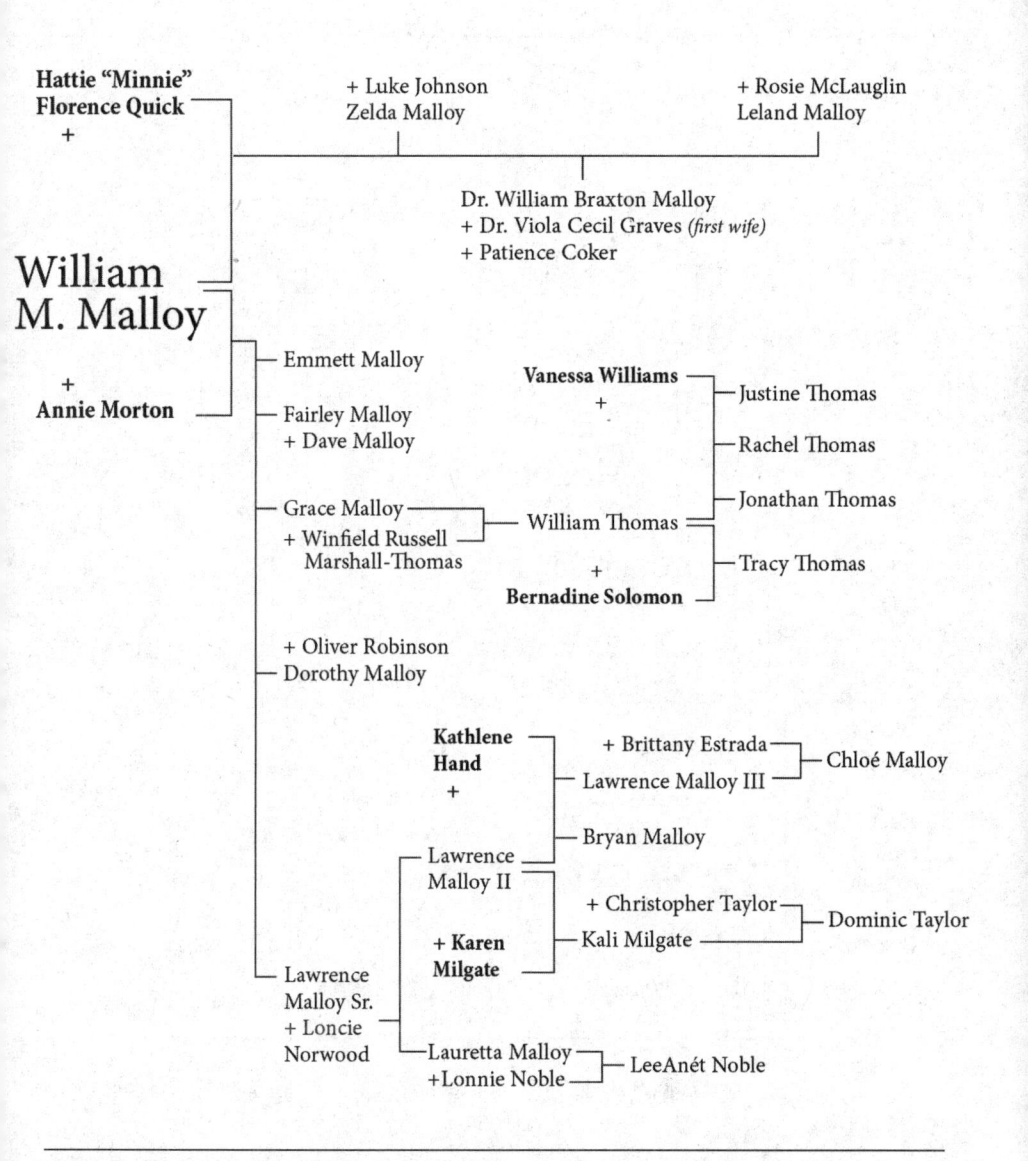

Hattie "Minnie" Florence Quick +

- \+ Luke Johnson / Zelda Malloy
- Dr. William Braxton Malloy
  - \+ Dr. Viola Cecil Graves *(first wife)*
  - \+ Patience Coker
- \+ Rosie McLauglin / Leland Malloy

William M. Malloy
+
Annie Morton

- Emmett Malloy
- Fairley Malloy
  - \+ Dave Malloy
- Grace Malloy
  - \+ Winfield Russell Marshall-Thomas
    - William Thomas = **Vanessa Williams** +
      - Justine Thomas
      - Rachel Thomas
      - Jonathan Thomas
      - Tracy Thomas
    - + **Bernadine Solomon**
- \+ Oliver Robinson / Dorothy Malloy
- Lawrence Malloy Sr.
  - \+ Loncie Norwood
    - Lawrence Malloy II
      - **Kathlene Hand** +
        - \+ Brittany Estrada / Lawrence Malloy III — Chloé Malloy
        - Bryan Malloy
      - \+ **Karen Milgate**
        - \+ Christopher Taylor / Kali Milgate — Dominic Taylor
    - Lauretta Malloy
      - +Lonnie Noble — LeeAnét Noble

This is the branch where my daughter and I reside via my father, who was the son of William M. Malloy and his second wife, Annie Morton.

Annie's Family

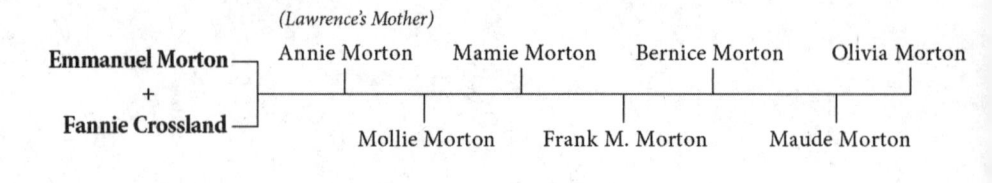

Emmanuel Morton + Fannie Crossland

- Annie Morton *(Lawrence's Mother)*
- Mollie Morton
- Mamie Morton
- Frank M. Morton
- Bernice Morton
- Maude Morton
- Olivia Morton

My father's mother's family, who were part of the displaced people of Indigenous tribes during the Trail of Tears.

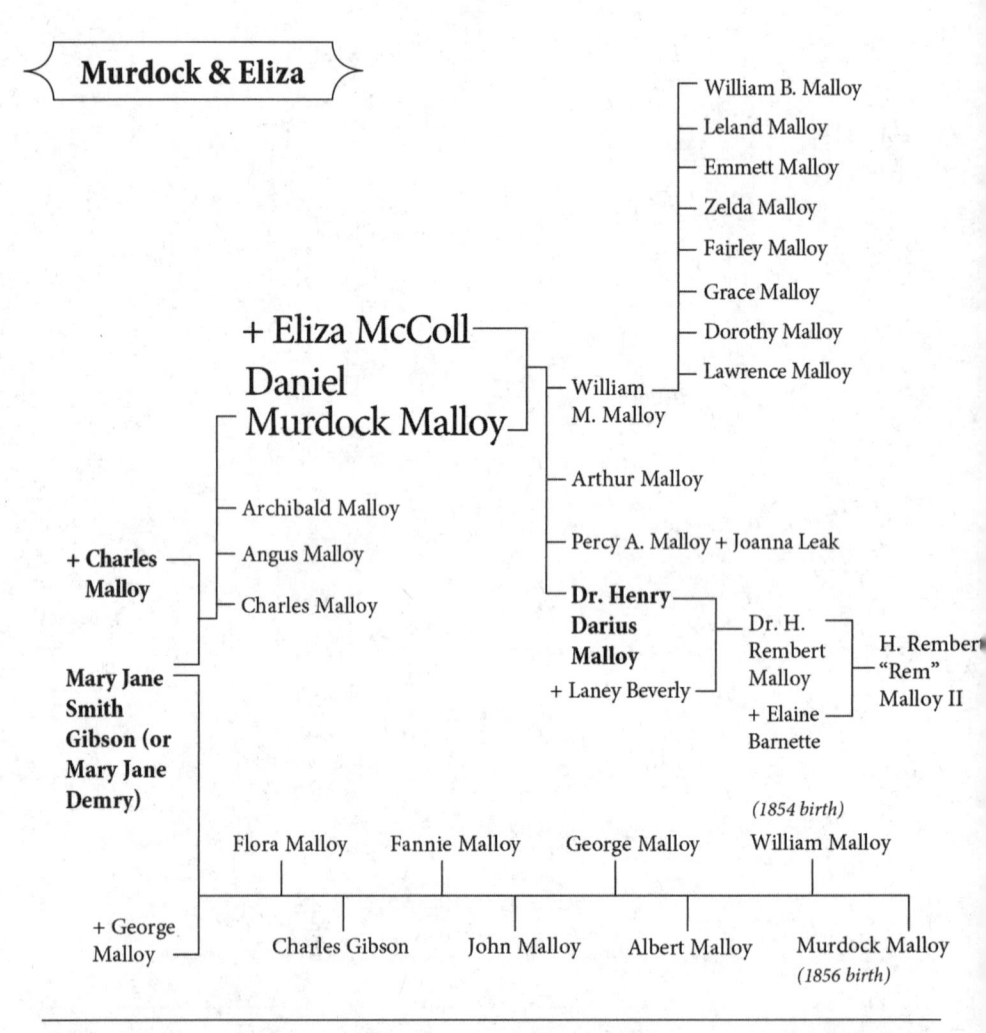

Murdock & Eliza

Daniel Murdock Malloy + Eliza McColl
- Archibald Malloy
- Angus Malloy
- Charles Malloy
- William M. Malloy
  - William B. Malloy
  - Leland Malloy
  - Emmett Malloy
  - Zelda Malloy
  - Fairley Malloy
  - Grace Malloy
  - Dorothy Malloy
  - Lawrence Malloy
- Arthur Malloy
- Percy A. Malloy + Joanna Leak
- Dr. Henry Darius Malloy + Laney Beverly
  - Dr. H. Rembert Malloy + Elaine Barnette
    - H. Rembert "Rem" Malloy II

+ Charles Malloy

Mary Jane Smith Gibson (or Mary Jane Demry)

+ George Malloy

- Flora Malloy
  - Charles Gibson
- Fannie Malloy
  - John Malloy
- George Malloy
  - Albert Malloy
- William Malloy *(1854 birth)*
  - Murdock Malloy *(1856 birth)*

After having Murdock and his siblings, Mary Jane Demry/Mary Jane Smith Gibson, the African seamstress, married George Malloy, who also worked for Charles Malloy (inheriting the last name), and started a new family.

William & Hattie

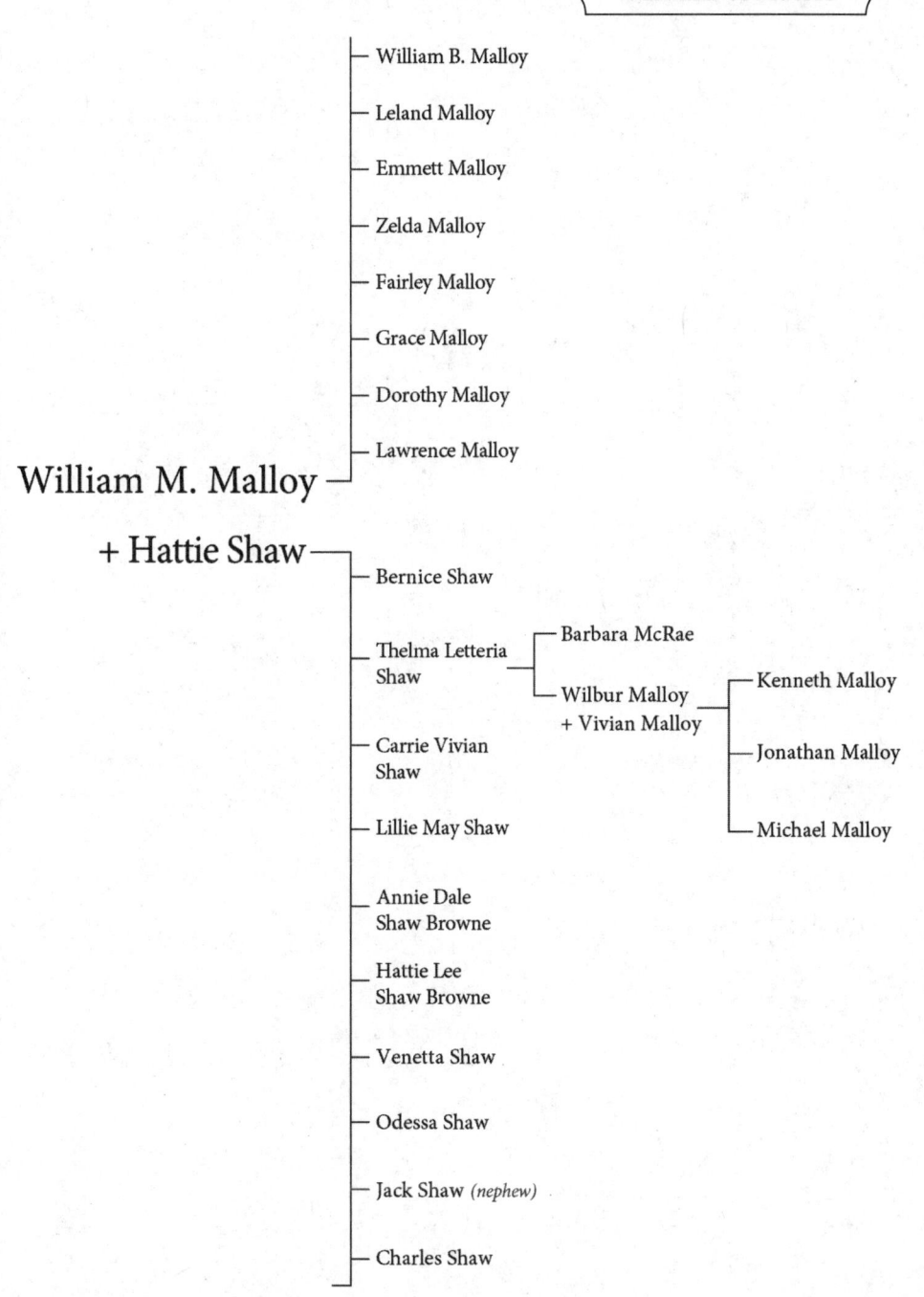

William M. Malloy + Hattie Shaw

- William B. Malloy
- Leland Malloy
- Emmett Malloy
- Zelda Malloy
- Fairley Malloy
- Grace Malloy
- Dorothy Malloy
- Lawrence Malloy

- Bernice Shaw
- Thelma Letteria Shaw
  - Barbara McRae
  - Wilbur Malloy + Vivian Malloy
    - Kenneth Malloy
    - Jonathan Malloy
    - Michael Malloy
- Carrie Vivian Shaw
- Lillie May Shaw
- Annie Dale Shaw Browne
- Hattie Lee Shaw Browne
- Venetta Shaw
- Odessa Shaw
- Jack Shaw *(nephew)*
- Charles Shaw

Hattie Shaw was well established before marrying William Murphy. She had children, as well as property to her name, and their marriage added many new relatives to the Malloy family. Here is one of our connections to Cousin Wilbur, as we are related twice.

Introduction

"When a tree falls in a lonely forest, and no animal is near by to hear it, does it make a sound?"

—Charles Riborg Mann and George Ransom Twiss, *Physics*

Lawrence Edward Malloy Sr. was a proud man who let everyone he crossed paths with know his story. This was how he kept the legacy of his family and their town, Laurinburg, North Carolina, alive.

He was also my father and LeeAnét's grandfather.

Laurinburg is in the southern part of the state, ten miles from the South Carolina border. Our family's significant accomplishments and sacrifices made there would be in vain if people stopped hearing their names.

In putting the puzzle of my family together as we shaped our lives, I was guided by my father's stories, even if subconsciously. His ambiguous answers to my direct questions as a child left me wondering what my father was *not* telling me. In the third grade at Kemp Mill Elementary School in our Maryland suburb, a classmate asked me about my freckles, which made me question my roots.

I asked my father about our origins.

Without a pause, Dad told me, with an unexpected sense of

INTRODUCTION

pride, "We are Scots." In the Black community, we typically do not speak on our white ancestry, which dates back to enslavement. This wasn't the same pride he displayed when he stood with his Alpha Phi Alpha fraternity brothers or when he talked about being Black as a prelude to a speech at an event. At my daughter's graduation parties, he would start his speeches with "As a Black man," and proceed to tell a story about his life, followed by a joke, before addressing the room. His statement of European identity was a confirmation of what we are but not who we are. This revelation opened a new world of discoveries for me, although his ninety-seven years on earth did not lend him an opportunity to fully share the story.

―

As a child, I was conscious of my family's status when we moved from a predominantly Black community to a predominantly white one. The Black community in River Terrace in Washington, DC, where we first lived, had an exodus of white residents when the Black community began to move in. My parents eventually settled in the Kemp Mill community of Silver Spring, Maryland, a suburb of Washington, DC. Our new yard and three-story home where I now had my own room had to mean we had a status shift. As stated in *The Color of Law* by Richard Rothstein, "President Kennedy's 1962 executive order attempted to end the financing of residential segregation by federal agencies."[1] We moved to Kemp Mill in 1964 as a result of Kennedy's executive order and other efforts to desegregate communities. While some neighborhoods offered incentives for Black people to move to their communities, the federal laws shifting neighborhoods also created sanctions to stop them. According to an

INTRODUCTION

article in *Washington Jewish Week,* about the history of the community, "Long and complicated racially restrictive covenants were used in Kemp Mill to exclude African Americans."[2]

Federal sanctions cropped up in many states. In 1948, even after the Supreme Court deemed segregated communities to be unconstitutional, discriminatory policies were still prevalent in deeds in Montgomery County, where we lived. In an article entitled "A Shameful Past," journalist Eugene L. Meyer gives one example: "No part of the land hereby conveyed shall ever be used, occupied by, sold, demised, transferred, conveyed unto, or in trust for, leased, or rented, or given to any negro or negroes, of any person or persons of negro blood or extraction, except that shall not be held to exclude partial occupancy of the premises by domestic servants of the grantee, his heirs and assigns."[3]

Also excluded were "any person of the Semitic race including Armenians, Jews, Hebrews, Persians, and Syrians." But if you had the finances and status, some selection committees would let you purchase a home anyway.

We were originally one of only two Black families in the community. When LeeAnét and I talked with some of our neighbors, they recalled the "welcome wagons" that would greet new Black homebuyers by driving by, screaming slurs, and targeting their homes with vandalism. This practice was prevalent when the Fair Housing Act was implemented in 1968, which on paper ended segregation and discriminatory sanctions.

Over time, our neighborhood grew more diverse, with the addition of Jewish people and other people of color. Amid the discrimination still taking place, people of different backgrounds in our community came together and celebrated each other: Jewish, Black, East Indian, Asian, and more. Prominent Black friends from the community included author Samuel F. Yette, Congressman Louis

INTRODUCTION

Stokes, renowned jazz musician Andy Goodrich, the Hughleys, Colonel James Hurd, civil rights activist Roscoe Nix, supermodel Gail Kendricks, the Harveys, and more. My parents embraced their neighbors, and the Gerstls, who lived across the street, are still dear friends who are like family.

My father served in World War II. After the war, he worked his way up in the federal government, beginning as a window clerk for the postal field service in 1948. By 1960, he was the managing editor and a writer for four US presidential cabinet members and the postmaster general's office, working with R. C. Stringer, Paul J. Cox, and James Thomason in the management branch, where he remained until 1965.[4] He made sure to document the names of his coworkers in his writings because he took great pride in his position.

In the late 1960s, he joined the staff at Howard University, working in treasury and then becoming the postmaster. He worked at Howard until about 1997. He retired several times, only to return again because he loved his work.

My mother, Loncie Malloy, also worked for the federal government. She was a supervisor in the Health, Education, and Welfare Department, where she focused on policy. She achieved GS-13, the third-highest pay grade. She enjoyed writing and would often write op-eds for Black publications. My daughter grew up seeing my mother's writings in *Jet* magazine with titles such as "Black Jobless Rate" that still resonate over thirty years after her death.[5]

In addition, she was a first soprano who worked with renowned artists such as Dr. Russell Woollen from the National Symphony Orchestra.

My father stood six foot two and slicked his hair back with

the help of Murray's Superior Pomade. My mother had curly sandy brown hair that she loved to highlight with red and sometimes blond streaks. She claimed to be an even five feet tall, but that was with a two-inch heel.

My father, Lawrence, was an alpha male, exuding confidence in his posture and his stance. He knew who he was and that he came from a special background. His proud presence was coupled with Southern charm: saying good morning, opening doors for women, and greeting others with a big smile. He and my mother were the life of every party. He took the dance floor with the same confidence with which he entered any room, and with a fearless demeanor, he made up his own moves; my mother did the same. They positioned themselves to make change, joining organizations such as the NAACP, taking major companies to court for discrimination, and donating to charities through the church and philanthropic groups like the Alpha Wives, which offers scholarships and mentorship to young Black students.

To me, my father felt omnipresent. He attended all my activities, and when my daughter was a child, teenager, and adult, he was there for her too, a constant presence at her plays and concerts. He supported her with money for college, all the while constantly instilling our family history in her.

This included painful memories. He was the youngest in his family, and the darkest family member. As a boy, he would have to enter stores through the back door, while his father, who could pass for white, was allowed across the tracks and in the front doors, not only because of his complexion but due to his status as a builder.

My father pressed on. When he was hospitalized, my daughter and I would serenade him with the songs he played and danced to on the stacked televisions in our living room.

INTRODUCTION

On March 14, 2014, I walked into Northwood Presbyterian Church in Silver Spring, Maryland, dreading "The Day." The space had been the church home of my mother and father since 1964. By joining this congregation, they helped integrate the suburban town of Kemp Mill. But on this day, the building was the calling ground for my father's funeral. With my daughter following in my steps, I passed his favorite pew and could hear my father's hearty laugh echoing through the sanctuary as it did when he would sit for hours after the service telling jokes to other parishioners.

This church was where my mother served as the only Black choir director, where I was one of three Black children in the choir, where I married my ex-husband at age nineteen, where my father never missed a service or an event. When my mother passed away twenty-eight years prior, my father became the one consistent force in my life.

Gathering my emotions, I inhaled and exhaled into the arms of Naomi Waddleton, a dear family friend. She and her husband, Preston "P. T." Waddleton, owned Action Oil and Action Limousine Company, which were used by almost every Black member of the community as well as the likes of Coretta Scott King and activist Dr. Dorothy Height.

After Mrs. Waddleton fixed my collar, I somehow made my way to the front pew. The pastor stepped forward and began to speak. I could not focus on her words until she said, "Lawrence had a lot of stories about growing up in the South; and though they were not true, we loved to hear them."

In that moment, all my daughter and I could see was red.

Now that his physical presence was gone, was this how he

INTRODUCTION

was going to be remembered, as a ninety-seven-year-old Black man spewing fairy tales for people's entertainment? I thought about the many stories he shared, and the receipts I witnessed and received proving his stories were factual—the same stories my daughter grew up with after my divorce when I moved back home in the early nineties. Everywhere he went, my father made sure his story was heard, a sort of compensation for the erasure and loss of his family's contributions to their community and society.

It wasn't just the pastor who didn't believe my father's stories: My own daughter had a hard time fathoming the lifestyle and contributions the family made in the years right after the Emancipation Proclamation was signed into law, giving many Black people their freedom from enslavement.

Before I could fully breathe, we were at the graveyard. During the burial, I watched through tear-filled eyes as the American flag floated in the air and landed on his casket. The soldier holding the trumpet couldn't get it to sound. My father's song could not be played, and his military honor came to a halt. We were never told why the horn would not blow.

Like that horn, our voices need to be heard. Lawrence E. Malloy Sr. constantly told his story, hoping someone would listen and take note. Was this muted horn a symbol that he would not be able to rest, or have comfort even after death, until his full truth was heard? After ninety-seven years on earth, his work was unfinished. Without his physical presence to guide me, I knew I had to feel his spirit and use his stories as connectors that would shift how we viewed history and ourselves as a family.

And so I began to unravel his words.

Over the past ten years, LeeAnét and I have seen and felt signs, messages, comments, and more, all of which triggered us

INTRODUCTION

to dig deeper into my father's stories, his life before us, and our bloodline. The signs were ubiquitous. One day, I walked into a building for a holiday event and someone asked, "Are you looking to trace your family?" Another time, as we struggled to find our uncle Leland in the records, we passed a street sign that said "Leland" in an area we frequented, yet we had never noticed his name. In our journey, guided by my father's words, we found the same people in his family listed as "Black," "White," "Mulatto," and "Colored" interchangeably according to the year, identifying race as a construct.

In December 2014, we visited the holiday exhibit at the Mormon temple in Maryland. The temple is a local landmark where people of all religions gather for the light show and world nativity exhibit, which is open to the public only a few times a year. There a guide told us: "Your ancestors are speaking to you." We were led to a research center that would become a major resource for our work.

The Church of Jesus Christ of Latter-Day Saints is known for maintaining in-depth census records. Now they have Black genealogy research clubs dedicated to tracing lost ancestry dating back to enslavement. We came across *The New York Age*, one of the most prominent African American newspapers of the nineteenth and early twentieth centuries, where prolific figures such as W. E. B. Du Bois had bylines.[6] Within those pages we discovered numerous articles about our family's daily life in Laurinburg, North Carolina.

In 1907, Booker T. Washington purchased *The New York Age* and named his long-time friend and associate Fred R. Moore as

INTRODUCTION

the editor and owner. *The New York Age*, a nationwide publication printed and based in New York City, would serve as a connector between Black communities and prominent families. From trending topics to updates on graduations and deaths, *The New York Age* reported it all.[7] This paper and numerous other Black newspapers helped the Malloys catch up on their familial affairs when away from home and today serve as resources for information about the family.

My father often spoke about his wealthy Black family, many of them doctors, living in a prosperous community during the Reconstruction period following the Civil War. From before 1863 and through 1877, the nadir of the era, his telling sounded like a fairy tale mixed with the nightmare of humans subjecting other humans to shameless acts of violence. It was the latter stories of prosperity that perhaps fueled statements like those made by the pastor at his funeral. Throughout his life, people questioned how a Black man could grow up with a silver spoon in his mouth during Reconstruction and in the segregated Jim Crow era.

Now I have proof that Laurinburg was one of those Black utopias in the South that were targeted by racists, like the 1921 massacre in Tulsa, Oklahoma, when a vibrant Black community perished at the hands of a violent racist mob. Hundreds were killed in Tulsa, and more than a thousand homes and countless businesses were destroyed. The proof about Laurinburg lies not only in newspapers, census reports, and other records, but most important, in my father's stories.

On a forbidding Southern swamp with streams that led to the waters of what was then Richmond County and later became Scotland County, a family, a people, and a community created their own garden of Eden, an oasis amid political chaos and dangerous gazes. Families whose parents were enslaved just

INTRODUCTION

a few years earlier built churches and businesses. The majority of these community members and entrepreneurs saw their hard-earned assets get ripped away. In 1904, famed educator Booker T. Washington sanctioned nearly two dozen of his disciples to create Laurinburg Institute to fight the remnants of a devastating political coup d'état, an insurrection that destroyed the careful progress made in Laurinburg. Local community members, Black and white, helped to acquire the land. Laurinburg Institute was built on a portion of land that the Malloy family owned and donated to the school.

"The Institute," as it is affectionately called, was responsible for the education of jazz musician Dizzy Gillespie, the families of director Spike Lee and actor Danny Glover, Sam Jones and dozens of other NBA basketball players, and thousands of college graduates in every field imaginable.

My father, his first cousin Henry Rembert Malloy, my mother, my daughter, my brother, and I all attended Howard University. The family from Laurinburg attended various other HBCUs, including Hampton University, Shaw University, Meharry Medical College, Johnson C. Smith University, and Barber-Scotia College.

During Reconstruction and part of the Jim Crow era, from the late nineteenth century to the mid-twentieth, Laurinburg and the Malloy home were hotspots for notable doctors, tennis players, and political figures. The town had spirit, and my father had tenacity.

Our research also led us to the first and only successful insurrection in US history, which started practically in our family's backyard.

Based on my father's stories and how he perceived his father's beginnings, which started the year enslavement ended, William

INTRODUCTION

Murphy Malloy, my grandfather, was residing in Laurinburg with his children when this insurrection took place.

By 1898, the Red Shirts had taken root in Laurinburg, beating and torturing any Black person they saw, as well as any white Republicans in the party of Lincoln. They continued their torture parade on the train to Wilmington, North Carolina, going on a killing rampage with Gatling guns and burning buildings and Black-owned businesses.

The harmonious ecosystem of the Black community was disrupted by a deep resentment that turned into fear and transformed into rage, mostly from Confederates still spiteful over a war they felt they won. Their goal was to diminish and separate the Black community into a newly created county and reverse any progress that had been made with white allies in the previous decades.

Activist and writer Tim Wise often speaks about how the terms *white* and *Black* were constructed to enshrine white supremacy.[8] The wealthy manipulated poor white people to fight against the Union by convincing them that Black people were their enemies. During the antebellum period, the early Democratic Party was for enslavement and represented Confederate pride and conservatism, while the early Republican Party was led by prominent abolitionists who fiercely opposed enslavement and provided as much opportunity as possible to free Black people, a practice that continued through Reconstruction. What the parties stood for would change over the years. Though my father's ancestors and their Black neighbors lost all the seats they held in the government, and the part of the county our family resided in was renamed Scotland County to separate the community by race, the town still persevered. My grandfather, boxed into a fight-or-flight environment, focused his attention on the education of his family and building generational wealth.

INTRODUCTION

The history of the town and my family extends to Scotland around the mid-eighteenth century. In 1715 the practice of enslavement was active in North Carolina, when Black people numbered 10,500 and white people numbered 6,500.[9] As time moved on, our relatives hid and faced kidnappers during enslavement, worked in the textile mills, and even became connected to the tragic Trail of Tears, where Indigenous people were slaughtered from 1830 to 1850.

Today, masses of people are seeking their ancestry by using DNA kits, hiring genealogists, or watching television series about finding their roots. All of us want to know who we are and where we come from. This is not easy. Pieces of our puzzle have been destroyed, many times on purpose. Now is the time to reconstruct these pieces to complete the picture. We need to hear about the people who triumphed amid chaos, who found ways to fight through generations by planting seeds that would continue to grow after they passed away. Now, more than ever before, we need to see a path to reinvent, to persevere, and to heal.

Although we lost my father, we did not want to see his stories buried with him, knowing the power they could have for generations to come. Today there is an intentional erasing of events that occurred after the Civil War through altering books and lessons in the South. Our family story is one we need to tell.

Our true story may help others understand how important it is to know yourself, to find yourself, to hold on to your legacy, and to not let anyone change or discredit your story. Growing up in a white suburb, I depended on my father's stories and the books I found in my mother's library to center me. Our story was not taught in school. Like many, I received an edited, copied-and-pasted version of history.

Our extended family's accomplishments, though noted, are

not common knowledge, nor are they celebrated, much like the town of Laurinburg itself, despite its historic Black wealth, its boarding school, and its racially diverse communities during Reconstruction.

We had no choice but to write this book.

When my daughter and I went viral in 2014 for bringing forty women of color to the Paris Fashion Week runway for Rick Owens's Spring/Summer women's line, shifting fashion to a focus on body positivity in an homage to Black sorority rituals, we were asked by the press about our connection to fashion. It was a full circle moment. My great-great-grandmother was a seamstress and servant during slavery. And as a teenager and young adult, my father, working for one of his father's businesses, provided cotton and fabric from the family company to New York's fashion district.

Though distanced from West Africa, the culture of passing down stories orally from griots, a designated class of people given the responsibility of protecting and sharing history, was in my father's blood.

When faced with consistent trauma, the amygdala that controls our emotional fire detector in the brain expands, puts us on edge, and causes anxiety. The only way to heal this wound is to be embraced, to be held, to be given comfort. I learned this through my studies in music therapy and in discussions with my daughter, who completed the Leader in Me training, which focuses on *The 7 Habits of Highly Effective People* by Stephen R. Covey. Reconnecting with my father's stories and understanding their possibilities helped my daughter and me through the grieving process, though the journey was paved with more thorns than I could imagine.

The erasure of our history and people continues to affect us.

INTRODUCTION

This erasure can initiate a traumatic domino effect. We must let the knowledge and experiences of our ancestors be the balm that binds the cuts so we can move forward together.

In the words spoken by a cousin at my father's funeral, "All of Lawrence's stories were true; the problem is you would not expect a Black man in America from his generation to have had such an experience."

1. AFRICANS, SCOTS, AND AMERICANS

My father embraced his Blackness as a badge of honor and resilience.

Growing up in Laurinburg, North Carolina, in the early twentieth century, he was surrounded by family, friends, and associates who were happy. It wasn't odd for the culture, but it was odd for anyone during that era to possess any level of positivity. In some ways, it was a mask covering the elephant in the room or trying to maintain the proverbial Southern charm. The sanctity of this community was to be protected at all costs. The landscape where they worked shifted from obscure swampland to a community of well-built homes, farmland, churches, and businesses surrounded by rivers, ponds, striped lawns, and cypress trees.

Now, my father and the entire town were aware of the horrific wear and tear of potential racial violence on the community's nerves, and they recognized the cost of constantly fighting physical threats. With white supremacist groups on the rise, attacking integrated businesses and more, they had to protect their mental state by filling the moments they could control with joy. The Black community's gatherings, sports, and church services provided a release. It was important to fight together against others, but not with one another.

Members of the Black community in Laurinburg, part of Stewartsville Township in Scotland County, knew not to compete with one another for jobs. Rather, they celebrated one another's successes. A win for one was a win for all. They didn't dare to shake or rattle the growth process. Laurinburg then was experiencing an evolving era of prosperity when Black families were allowed to become landowners and to run their own businesses and farms. The township knew what their families offered and gave to the larger community. This is what surrounded Lawrence as a child, and what his father experienced during the height of Reconstruction: a sense of community, resilience, and excellence that would remain with them for the rest of their lives.

Much like the community, Lawrence's personality and traditions were influenced by the blend of cultures he was exposed to and the DNA in his cells. In Laurinburg, Black residents walked on streets with Scottish names. Immigrants from Scotland came to the area in the eighteenth and nineteenth century, some heeding the call of land and opportunities while others were escaping the harsh consequences of sheep stealing, English taxes, and the church.[1] They brought a diverse range of inventions to America, contributing to the culture with sewing machines, fiddles, bagpipes, and flutes. In the twentieth century, the town hosted traditions from both Black and Scottish cultures, such as eating soul food and playing Highland Games. Some of my father's friends spoke Gaelic, and everyone used the same Southern terms. Dizzy Gillespie spoke so often about enslaved people who spoke Gaelic and growing up with Black friends who spoke the language in North Carolina that he inspired others to research the topic.[2] There were other staples popular in Laurinburg among the entire community as well, such as persimmon beer.[3] Both white and Black residents gathered at the beer garden my father managed as a teen.

West African culture was brought to North Carolina and infused with the American one developed on plantations and in communities of free Black people. The culture brought from Scotland by thousands of immigrants spread throughout the pre-existing Black culture and that of the Indigenous tribes. In addition to Scottish foods such as salted porridge, the Scottish brought the Presbyterian religion, which became a central force in the local community of Black and white residents.

The fiddle was embraced during the eighteenth and nineteenth centuries, and traveling Black musicians often performed professionally throughout North Carolina. In the 1840s and 1850s, the first known Black professional performer, Juba (known as the inventor of tap dance), spent time with Irish-Scotch dancers at integrated music gatherings in New York. He fused the Irish forms of dance with African footwork and would challenge both Black and white dancers as he traveled the world performing. His quick movements and style going toe to toe with his white counterparts resulted in him winning each dance challenge. This dance form was also prominent in the South, with a flat-foot style of movement.

Most of the Black and white residents of Laurinburg were descendants of Scotland. Some Black people were proud of their Scottish heritage, while others acknowledged only their Black heritage with pride.

On any given day, whether asked for a story or not, Lawrence would stretch his arms with the exclamation "Oh, me," which my daughter LeeAnét interpreted as "Old me." As an infant listening to his stories, she often referred to him as "Damnpa." My mother would exclaim how cute she was to pronounce her granddaddy's name that way.

In his next breath, he would change his voice to an earth-rattling vibrato, emulating a pastor in an old wooden church where the acoustics sent echoes bouncing from wall to wall. My father would yell, "A white man from Scotland and a Black woman got together and had a child! To protect them, a town was built, and that is where the first Black Malloy resided, in Richmond County, North Carolina!" What would follow was a detailed account of our family history.

On other occasions, when checking out at the grocery store, for example, he would greet a new cashier with a smile and say, "Do you know who I am? I'm a Malloy. We owned one of the largest fabric and construction companies. My family built a town to protect each other!"

The cashier would smile and engage. At every visit, Lawrence would add more to the story. Later, when I would visit the same store, the cashier would tell me, "I just saw your father. I didn't know there were that many Black doctors in the South back then!" I'm sure those cashiers passed the stories down to people they knew.

Or my father would lean back on the sofa in the living room with the telephone to his ear and say, "My daddy was a white man, and his daddy was a Scottish man who married a Black woman. They could pass for white people." These introductions would lead to at least an hour-long monologue. At the end of the call, my daughter and I would ask who he was talking to, since the conversation had shifted into the banter you might hear when my father talked to an old family friend. And he would say it was the phone company representative.

His stories drew people in. I found out from my daughter that when teachers asked for my number, she would give them his number instead, knowing he would tell the teacher a story. She mentioned that one teacher said the next day in class: "I loved learning about your family. Now I actually need to speak to your mother!"

Lawrence's grandfather was Daniel Murdock Malloy, born around 1844. Our father seldom mentioned him other than referring to "Murdock's house" while telling a story about his grandmother Eliza's family. My father's grandparents were stern and took on their role as elders with the utmost dignity. Eliza, also born in 1844, had signature long black hair that fell well below her shoulders; my father mentioned this about Eliza every time he spoke about her. He only met her a few times, so her physical features encompassed much of what he knew of her. Meeting grandparents or great-aunts and great-uncles was a rare event in this era when so many were displaced during enslavement and the Civil War.

Before he met Eliza, as a young man Daniel walked the unpaved roads of Laurel Hill, North Carolina, a safe place in Richmond County for Black and mixed-race people, which was necessary because of the abuse and hardships of that era. This community encompassed parts of what is now Laurinburg. Daniel was the son of Charles Malloy, a Scottish man born in 1810 who helped industrialize North Carolina.

During Daniel's childhood, members of the Black community were forced into harsh labor, often farming, picking cotton and tobacco, or detasseling corn while fending off dangerous heat, snakes, and field rats, or tending to the homes of their enslavers. At the same time, groups of freedmen worked as blacksmiths, farmers, cobblers, artisans, and more. In the Northeast, many Black freedmen were allowed to vote. They started newspapers, owned businesses, formed literary societies, attended the opera and piano recitals, and were outspoken about the horrors and inhumanity of enslavement. This was not the case in the South, however, due to the large number of Confederates. Freedmen had to be cautious and strategic about how they progressed in society.

Daniel was listed in the census and other reports as "mulatto" in 1870, as "black" in 1895, and as "white" in 1912. The term *mulatto* had origins dating back to the sixteenth century and derived from the Latin word *mula*, a term for a cross between a donkey and a horse. It was a new term in the Black community, and yet it appeared in the census for decades. No matter what the trend became in years to come, no Malloys ever referred to themselves as mixed or mulatto. The one-drop rule was the standard: If you had one drop of Black blood, you were Black. This rule remained prevalent in the white and Black communities for decades. It served to keep children from receiving any inheritance or asserting any right to their white parent's assets.

Daniel was trained in farming and worked in the local mill, and he was able to benefit from both. He would eventually provide for his family, using these funds to set up his children for success with training that led to good business acumen and future income.

———

I had to be meticulous in gathering the details of the family while researching our history. My father's stories and endless references were the guide when the census showed numerous people of the same name. Several Charles Malloys appear in the 1870 census, but cross-referencing family trees and timelines allowed me to follow the correct path and person. It would be easy for anyone to mix up a story, using only the census. I found two Daniel Murdock Malloys in the same census. After further research I found the one born in 1844 was Daniel Murdock, my relative. The other was born in 1857 in the same extended family. But the latter Daniel Murdock had a father named George, as well as a different address and resident number, the count of people living at the residence, on a different page in the 1870 census. Details such as these helped guide my steps.

These small discrepancies within documentation opened big doors for LeeAnét and me while investigating the history of our family. Although many people named their children after their favorite family member, person, or ancestor, mostly to honor and pridefully carry on their name, in this case the doubling of names had deeper repercussions. I found other households jumbled with my family who didn't previously live together. Later I would discover many tactics were used by various sources to halt Black descendants from connecting to white relatives.

In the 1800s, many people—both Black and white—took the names of the royal families in Scotland, mimicking their culture in an effort to reflect a perceived higher status. If you were named after royalty and possessed the last name of a wealthy family, success and assimilation into society would be easier.

At first, these practices were fun, like enslaved people gathering for cakewalk dances to imitate the way white slave owners and others put on airs to pretend that they were royal. The same old names just circled about the town, making spelling and reading them easier. Not everyone saw the value of education, and only those who could afford it attended school.

North Carolina was a popular destination for Scottish immigrants in the eighteenth century due to the many economic benefits offered to Highland Scots by Gabriel Johnston, the royal governor of North Carolina from 1734 to 1752.[4]

In 1774, twenty thousand Scottish immigrants came to America. By 1790, there were populations and communities of Black people and Scots of varied statuses throughout North Carolina. Due to the large number of Scottish immigrants at that time, legislation was passed in Parliament in 1803 called the Passenger Vessels Act. The new law regulated the conditions of the ships and imposed fees on immigrants, which hindered impoverished Highlanders from traveling to the States.[5] Enslavement in Scotland ended in 1833. It was ahead of the United States in recognizing the inhumanity of chattel enslavement. Beginning in 1846, larger groups of Scottish immigrants traveled to America as a result of the Highland Potato Famine. Famine resulting from diseased potato crops killed up to 25 percent of the Scottish population and forced many people to seek refuge in other countries.[6]

The journey from Argyll, Scotland, to North Carolina in the eighteenth and nineteenth centuries was a rigorous one for the Presbyterian Scots who were looking for a way out of poverty, and they risked their lives for a chance at a better one. The trip took three months, typically in massive, dark, and damp sailing vessels. Many did not survive the trip, as seasickness overcame the travelers early in the voyage.

In the 1830s, Charles Malloy, his wife, and their children, along with his Black seamstress/lover and their children, traveled from Scotland. After a journey full of much despair and hardship, it felt like defeat when they were met head-on with violence once again in the United States because of the human slave trade.

In North Carolina, Charles Malloy used water to create the

energy necessary to fuel his mill as early as 1835. This power source enabled the mill to surge beyond its competitors, outperforming them and providing a primary source of income for the family. In addition, Charles built Presbyterian churches. This religion remained central for both white and Black Malloys in the generations that followed.

In the late 1840s, Charles moved his seamstress/lover and their children, including Daniel Murdock, who was born in 1844, back to Scotland, leaving his wife and other children in North Carolina. In Scotland, formerly enslaved Black people were starting their lives with the basic rights they had been denied in the United States for generations. However, around 1850, lured by greater opportunity in America, Charles and his mistress, as well as their children, returned to the United States. They traveled as a white family because, by law, any free Black person from another country had to return to that country after three months. The Malloys' experience of traveling to America differed from that of African people who were brought over in chains without knowing the language or what awaited them in the States. They landed in Cross Creek, North Carolina, rejoining Charles's wife and children. Increased land rents and taxes in Scotland had caused discord there.[7] In North Carolina, this was not their worry: Johnston's programs that provided incentives for Scottish immigrants in the form of tax breaks and land grants had continued with some revisions. In the new country, the Malloys sought to build a better life.

Charles would later free Daniel's mother, who remained with him after regaining her freedom. It appears other white and white-passing Malloys also practiced manumissions, buying enslaved people in order to free them. The practice of manumissions allowed the like of Benjamin Banneker, the African

American mathematician and astronomer, to live as a free man. Banneker's grandfather was bought by his white grandmother, herself an indentured servant. She freed him so that they could live together as a couple. During our research, we learned that we were related to Banneker on the Morton side of his family.

Articles about the first Malloys in North Carolina suggest that the family hired enslaved people and paid them as workers. The documentation alludes to this being a favorable process and example for neighbors, since wealthy families were not commonly challenged in a town they funded. Due to their financial status, the Malloys did not have to follow the harsh norms of society. When Charles passed away in 1891, few Union sympathizers held his level of wealth in the local community.

The names of Daniel's mother and Charles's wife were hard to find. It's possible that Daniel's mother—the Black seamstress whom Charles freed yet kept with him—had other owners and later husbands, resulting in a change of surnames.

The seamstress might have been a Mary Jane Smith Gibson, who was listed on the 1900 census with a birth year between 1820 and 1829, or a Mary Demery, who is on the family tree of a distant cousin. At the time, there were, of course, many women with the name Mary. They were named after the Queen of Scotland or the Virgin Mary.

Due to the status of women in this era, they were often referred to by their titles or roles, such as seamstress, wife, or servant. Their identity in the eyes of others focused on what they did rather than who they were. One could argue that these two facets were interchangeable for women in the early nineteenth century. Though Charles Malloy was distanced from his Black descendants in the generations that followed, this practice of coverture, the laws that deemed women to be under the authority of their husbands as their property, would remain.

In the same household with Charles's wife and their children lived Daniel's mother and her children by Charles. While creating one home of two worlds in Black and white, Charles Malloy kept up his travels, bringing back tools and items from Scotland, creating streams of income, buying land, and starting companies in North Carolina.

Charles's family and those of his workers would have been instant targets upon their return to the States. Having a close association with Black people put the entire family in danger.

Charles had to hide the identity of his Black children. The land he developed in Laurel Hill served as a safe space for them to live. It would also serve as a space for other Black and mixed-race families hiding from slave catchers.

During Daniel's childhood, though enslavement touched every corner of the plantations and the hidden free communities, a vibrant culture still developed. The release offered by singing and dancing and eating meals together allowed Black residents to live with hope amid deplorable conditions. Since the enslaved Africans were not allowed to bring any part of their culture with them to the New World, they found creative ways to hide their traditions and important items during the Middle Passage. For example, native herbs and seeds were braided into the hair.[8] Holding on to recipes by sharing them verbally was another method. Songs had hidden messages and were used as a tool of communication. This wasn't a one-size-fits-all culture: Some enslaved people risked their life to escape, while others took their own lives to do the same.

Though Charles was financially stable, Daniel had to farm to support himself. He had to learn the ways of the land to make sure he was able to prosper. While still a child, he could not afford to be childlike. Being noticed as a Black boy outside of his central community could result in his being captured and enslaved. He had to learn the muddy roads that took him home, the roads that led to danger, how to survive alone, and how to live a sustainable life on the farm.

During the Civil War, which began in 1861, some groups of Southern enslaved people refused to work. Plantation owners had to bargain with them and offer wages to keep their farms running. When Union soldiers showed up at some plantations, they would discover that the white people had fled, leaving enslaved people behind. In other areas, the plantations were completely deserted. There was a movement in place to end enslavement and to provide reparations, a campaign promoted by Union soldiers, the Black community, abolitionists, and Union sympathizers.

During the war, in addition to fighting alongside and aiding Union soldiers, the Malloy family's focus was on keeping their crops, surviving, and helping their neighbors, without knowing what the end of the war would mean for people of color. Union general William Tecumseh Sherman recruited the people he spared, and those recruits, plus Black Union soldiers, went on to repair bridges and wagons, reconstruct torn-down properties, and carry and transport the goods that the Union army confiscated from the Confederates.

———

In Laurel Hill, Daniel met Eliza McColl, another Black transplant seeking respite on Malloy land. Eliza came from wealth, and her parents were willing to sacrifice for her safety. She hailed from

Marlboro County, South Carolina, by way of Alabama, where her family owned acres of farmland. Her white father, seeking refuge for his Black daughter, bought land in Laurel Hill where she could live safely. He put the deed in her name to ensure her freedom and to protect her from the Fugitive Slave Act of 1840 and the slave catchers who targeted free Black people and forced them back into enslavement.[9] This was a common practice, again akin to the life of Benjamin Banneker, who was deeded land at age six in the 1700s.

During her childhood, Eliza was surrounded by racism. However, in her home, she was well taken care of, and she was listed as white in the census reports. Once of age, around fourteen in that era, she was displaced and could not publicly be seen as part of her family, only as a Black woman and worker. This put an instant target on her back.

Once an adult, she was confronted with what the world was and its collective disdain for who she was. Marlboro County was the only world she knew. Today we can click a button and see what life is like in a faraway place like Africa. In the 1840s, there were only hints that free communities and towns even existed. News of these places spread by word of mouth. Eliza knew only of Southern towns where Black people were forced to be subservient. Laurel Hill was something different.

In those days, in a community based on commerce, love and romance were contingent upon status and financial gain. One's income needed to be reinvested in the community. Building self-sustaining wealth was essential for survival. Daniel was born into wealth but did not refrain from hard work. He tilled his own land. Though building wealth was a focus, protecting family was of even greater importance. The father and husband's duty was to provide and make sure the family had all of its needs met, and the Malloy men took this duty to heart. They were known to be soft-natured, generous gentlemen with power. Their close neighbors were kind and giving as well. This stance was connected to their deep study of the Bible and their church attendance.

Daniel and Eliza were courting and married during the war. As the war came to an end in 1865, the community grew. The 1866 census, the first after Daniel and Eliza's marriage several years earlier, listed Eliza as white. Daniel and Eliza eventually started a family, which would grow to include five boys.

The Civil War brought about division in the South and within the Malloy family, as white Malloys fought for both the Union and the Confederacy. Charles had a gun factory that manufactured guns for the war. Though North Carolina had joined the Confederacy, thousands of residents were secret Union sympathizers. Charles was a Confederate who turned sympathizer for the Union. The woods surrounding the man-made lake Charles built served as a hiding place for soldiers who faced General William Tecumseh Sherman's onslaught. He turned over his products to General Sherman to be spared fires set by the Union Army, which was winning the war.[10] Though their properties were spared, some fires did break out in the Malloys' backyards.

After the war ended and enslavement was abolished by the Thirteenth Amendment on December 6, 1865, celebrations sprang up across the United States that included both Black and white people who felt aligned due to their work as indentured slaves.[11] Among the many areas affected by the war were those near the Lumbee River, the Pee Dee River, and the Santee River, where many of the Black members of the Malloy family lived. From those places, the Malloys spread out to the nearby communities of Fayetteville, which was forty miles northeast of Laurinburg, and Chapel Hill, Raleigh, and Durham, North Carolina. No matter their location, they supported the Union.

Through the census, which was recorded every ten years beginning in 1790, we have records of Native Americans in our family living with their Black relatives. They were also listed as Cherokee freedmen in the *Enrollment Cards for the Five Civilized Tribes*. My cousin Wilbur Malloy, who grew up in Laurinburg in the late forties and fifties, told me about a law created to stop Native Americans and Black people from marrying each other so they couldn't produce children and outnumber the white people in the town. North Carolina was one of three states to create statutes against miscegenation between the Black and Native communities.

Lawyer and lecturer Andrew D. Weinberger listed a few of the state statutes in a 1957 article for the *Journal of Negro Education*.[12] According to Appalachian State University's Digital Scholarship and Initiatives annotation of the article, the first miscegenation statute dates back to 1887 and was entitled "An act to amend section one thousand eight hundred and ten of The Code." The North Carolina law read, "All marriages between an Indian and a Negro or between an Indian and a person of Negro descent to the third generation inclusive shall be utterly void. *Provided*, this act shall only apply to the Croatan Indians. [Note: Croatan was the tribal name for the Lumbee at this time.] A later statute . . . provides that intermarriage between a Cherokee Indian of Robeson County and a Negro or person of Negro descent to the third generation is prohibited. . . . [Note: Cherokee Indians of Robeson County was the tribal name for the Lumbee at this time.] This statute sounds as if it merely updates the 1887 law to reflect the change in the tribal name."[13] These laws were part of a series of Jim Crow laws focused on miscegenation, which continued until *Loving v. Virginia* in 1967, which made interracial marriage legal.

After the Civil War ended, the central Presbyterian Church allowed select Black people to attend service with those who enslaved them. Previously, access had been limited to the small balcony at the top of the church. Now Black residents could build their own churches.

———

The Reconstruction Acts slowly started to initiate progress in 1867. Even before the war ended, President Abraham Lincoln, the Republicans, and others who were considered "radical" advocated for giving Confederate land in the South to Black families. In 1865, proponents of Reconstruction worked to figure out ways to promote equality and to help the formerly enslaved join society. As stated on the United States Senate website, "The Reconstruction Act of 1867 outlined the terms for readmission to representation of rebel states. The bill divided the former Confederate states, except for Tennessee, into five military districts. Each state was required to write a new constitution, which needed to be approved by a majority of voters—including African Americans—in that state. In addition, each state was required to ratify the Fourteenth Amendment to the Constitution. After meeting these criteria related to protecting the rights of African Americans and their property, the former Confederate states could gain full recognition and federal representation in Congress. The act became law on March 2, 1867, after Congress overrode a presidential veto. Admission to representation of the former Confederate states began the next year, with Arkansas leading the way."[14] At the same time, there was a glimmer of hope among the Malloy family, as that year also brought the blessing of a new Malloy heir.

2. 1865

My father's love for his hometowns of Laurinburg and Laurel Hill ran so deep that he made sure my name was spelled "Lauretta" versus the common spelling "Loretta." My friends to this day recall how he pronounced it, elongating the "Lau" phonetically and calling out my name in his Southern accent. One of his other deep loves, in addition to his wife and children, was that for his father.

He would often say, "My daddy was a white man," a statement that confused my daughter and me because we are Black. In one breath he would talk about the travesties his family experienced at the hands of the white man, followed by how great his father—whom he referred to as "a white man"—was. My grandfather, a sandy-haired man we only saw in photos, did not resemble what we considered to be a white man. My father wasn't bragging about his proximity to whiteness; his statement spoke to his father William's access to and ability to navigate both of the worlds he lived in.

A mirror in our home has long displayed photos from important events in our lives. I've displayed pictures from my work as an assistant to Quincy Jones and as the talent coordinator for the first Clinton inauguration; with Whitney Houston; at my daughter's dance performances and experiences with Broadway stars such as Baakari Wilder; and from my work in journalism interviewing Brandy and Babyface, among others, with my daughter by my side as a teen journalist.

Although one of his best friends was a white lawyer whose house was adjacent to ours, my father reacted strongly if triggered when he saw a white face on the mirror decorated by my daughter and me. Immediately, he would flash back and remind us how supremacist groups treated people of color. When he spoke, my father's usual smile shifted to an angry grimace, and his voice growled as he took the photos off the mirror. And yet, he always talked about his own father, "a white man," with the highest regard.

Following in the rituals his father taught him, every morning, from the top of his lungs, amplified by the echo of the shower, my father would sing the refrain of Hattie E. Buell's 1877 hymn with more passion than a Southern Baptist preacher at offering time: "I'm a child of the King, I'm a child of the King, Jesus is my Savior, I'm a child of the King."[1] His North Carolina dialect blared out every "King" as "Kane" before switching to the Lord's Prayer as he got dressed in one of the hundreds of suits that filled more than one closet. (He saved the white suits for dances, as they matched his white Cadillac.) This was my morning soundtrack on the top floor of our home in the mid-nineties. His song and prayer were rooted in his childhood, and I knew better than to interrupt him before he was finished.

When my father spoke about his daddy and how much William did for him, this six-foot-three man would instantly break into tears. His cries were audible moans. "My daddy was a great man, he taught me everything, he was a great man," he would blurt out as he cried. My father was never afraid to shed a tear. He wasn't a fearful man and would quickly tell you he was a prizefighter during his army days and knew how to use a rifle from his teen years.

If I or my daughter ever talked back to my father, he'd say, "I could never talk to my daddy like that." Then he'd tell us that he had to call his father "sir" and that William never spared the rod. Fear and safety were instilled in my father much like in Christianity: He feared his father, but at the same time he knew William would protect him and take care of his needs.

My grandfather lived a long life for someone born in the mid-nineteenth century, dying in his nineties. My parents had me in their late thirties and forties, and I never met him. Looking at his photos, it is hard to decipher his personality. My image of him was formed by my father's stories and my imagination. I figured he stood seven feet tall and that his life was solely dedicated to traditional fatherly duties.

He never wore a smile in any photo. This was perhaps stemming from Frederick Douglass's admonition to Black people to always present ourselves in photos with dignity, to combat stereotypes of minstrelsy.

As I learned during my social psychology studies under Dr. Ralph Gomes, the founder of the only PhD sociology program at an HBCU, early psychiatrists examined runaway enslaved people who were demonized as criminals. In 1851, physician Samuel Cartwright created the term drapetomania, a disease that made enslaved people want to run away; he also claimed Black people with too much freedom had mental abnormalities.[2] This was well before G. Stanley Hall founded the first psychology laboratory in the United States at Harvard in 1883.[3] Cartwright's diagnoses were later deemed racist and unfounded.

Another former professor, Dr. Hope Hill, currently in the psychology department at Howard University, has researched the effects that violent environments have on Black children and the beneficial effects of having social, community, and parental support. Her 1996 article in the *Journal of Child and Family Studies* highlights the improvement of environmental trauma-induced anxiety in Black children when the parents and community intervene.[4] Though the children of Laurinburg were exposed to violence, they also received a supportive embrace from their families and the community at large, which reduced their levels of anxiety.

After the Civil War, many Black people wanted to integrate into the larger society quickly. When asked, some would claim that they were never enslaved and came from a free family. This wasn't a form of denial, but rather a tactic for survival. There were many wealthy Black people throughout the United States in the 1800s: Some were self-made, and some had inherited land and wealth. The need to help one another wasn't just preached in sermons; it was embedded in the Black community with few exceptions.

The end of enslavement created new classes of Black people. Those who had their freedom prior to the war could focus on establishing themselves, while others felt they had no choice but to return to sharecropping. In the post–Civil War period, the Black Malloys included Daniel and Eliza and their children; Daniel's mother's children, with Charles and from other marriages; and some who had been enslaved by the Malloys and took on the name. The different branches of the family lived in different parts of North Carolina and knew of each other; some were close, and others didn't get along. My father would often say, "All Malloys are related."

Daniel and Eliza lived on acres of land with a home that had servants' quarters. Daniel had an amazing talent for growing crops. It was as if he had a magical serum that caused fruits and vegetables to sprout like weeds. In fact, in census documents on Ancestry.com, he's portrayed as being well known for his crops. He was paid well, selling them to the community and keeping his family fed. Folks came from all over to purchase from him.

In 1865, Daniel and Eliza had their second baby boy, William Murphy Malloy. His brother James Malloy was three years older. My grandfather was initially listed in the census as white under the spelling of "Malley," then later listed as a mulatto under "Malloy" as a young boy in North Carolina. Given that birth certificates weren't available until 1898, we go by my father's stories and knowledge of his father's birth year.[5]

Three Black communities evolved in this era, some better than others in entrepreneurship and building their economy, including Cross Creek, where many Malloys went after living in Scotland County and remained; Stewartsville; and Washington Park. All these communities were mixtures of Scottish, Irish, Indigenous, and African residents. Laurel Hill and Laurinburg can be considered part of the Deep South. John and Dale Reed, authors of *1001 Things Everyone Should Know About the South*, define the Deep South as "an area roughly coextensive with the old cotton belt, from eastern North Carolina through South Carolina, west into East Texas, with extensions north and south along the Mississippi."[6] The towns in this region were heavily affected by the Civil War.

———

In *Black Reconstruction in America*, W. E. B. Du Bois describes the strikes started by the enslaved in the South and how they acted as a major catalyst for the Union winning the war.[7] The fight was happening in the fields and in the homes. This is a piece of history we rarely hear discussed.

According to the 1863 Bureau of Colored Troops, 179,000 Black soldiers fought in the Civil War for the Union, as did Asian and Indigenous people.[8] The Black soldiers made up ten percent of the Union soldiers. The Indigenous and Asian soldiers typically had noncombatant roles. The majority of the Black soldiers were part of a specially formed unit, the United States Colored Troops (USCT). It was a proud honor for most to serve the Union during the war. Black soldiers pushed through and when allowed to have weapons were often given low quality guns in comparison to others.

The fight against enslavement was multifaceted and consisted of all walks of life. In *Black Women Abolitionists*, Shirley J. Yee writes about the many societies of Black women abolitionists that exploded across the United States, leading the way for abolitionist societies composed of other groups.[9] Frederick Douglass advised President Lincoln, who took his thoughts under consideration. Martin R. Delany, the only Black man to become a major during the Civil War, and ardent abolitionists like John Brown were vital to the Emancipation movement.

Brown risked his life while successfully freeing twenty-five hundred enslaved people, bringing them to freedom through daring invasions. In 1859, he raided the federal arsenal in Harpers Ferry, Virginia, hoping that the local enslaved people would join his revolt. He was convicted of treason and hanged on December 2, 1859.[10]

The burgeoning Reconstruction movement was eyed with cautious optimism. Dr. Henry Louis Gates Jr. said, "Reconstruction revealed a fact that had been true but not always acknowledged even before the Civil War: that it was entirely possible for many in the country, even abolitionists, to detest slavery to the extent that they would be willing to die for its abolition, yet at the same time to detest the enslaved and the formerly enslaved with equal passion. As Frederick Douglass said, 'Opposing slavery and hating its victims has become a very common form of abolitionism.'"[11]

Laurel Hill continued to flourish during my grandfather William's childhood. On Main Street, there was a general store and a post office as well as the mill, a railroad, and a depot. Richmond County, as it was called at the time, was where most of the Black community resided. The Presbyterian Church remained a staple of the community. Decades later, I would be married, and my daughter would be christened, in the Presbyterian Church, along with the majority of the Black community in our Washington, DC, suburb.

In 1850, the population of Laurel Hill was about 1,125. At the time, North Carolina had 869,039 people overall. In Richmond County in the 1860s, the population was 11,009. In North Carolina in 1860, there were between 100,000 and 500,000 Black people versus 1 million to 3 million in 1990.[12] This shows the drastic change that occurred in the North Carolina population after the Great Migration. These are the numbers on record, but Black people were rarely fully counted in the census during the nineteenth century.

During the Civil War, 40,000 Black soldiers died. Homes were abandoned, land was lost, and some moved in with relatives who still had homes and land. In Richmond County, families like the Malloys had passed down their land, which had been acquired through purchased land, Scottish ancestors who were given land, and grants and programs such as the 1862 Homestead Act, which gave immigrants, women, and more the opportunity to own land. In 1866 the Homestead Act was guaranteed for Black people as well.[13]

In 1869, Charles Malloy's mill was producing fabric and cotton that was sold throughout the thirty-three states. Charles owned over two thousand acres of land in eastern Richmond County before and after the Civil War. The mill was a major landmark of the county.

Four years later, a financial panic sent the industrial world reeling, with the onset of a depression that would last for years. It began with a stock market crash in Europe, then spread to the United States as European investors backed away from major American commitments such as railroads. This panic closed the Freedman's Bank in 1874, which had been created to build and protect Black wealth.

The Malloy family, Black and white, still worked at the mill. This was one of the few consistent methods of employment, similar to factories in the region in the twentieth century. Mill work in general was very hard on the body and often dangerous. An article in the *Wilmington Messenger* in 1896 reported that George

Malloy, a young Black man, was caught in the machinery at a cotton seed oil mill and mangled to death.

With the financial panic and the stress of the day-to-day managing of the mill, Charles sought ways to disengage and earn money instead as an investor. A former worker stepped up and bought shares in the mill, knowing this was a desperate time for families and most industries. The new partner was not as conservative as Charles.

Scholars argue that Charles's mill was a new capitalist model for local industry in a bereft town.[14] Cotton, produce, and other goods were selling at a fraction of the previous price. Setting the family up with a stream of income from the water-based mill by selling shares and taking on a partner gave the entire family access to new resources.

The mill flourished under its new capitalist model, but Charles was no longer at the helm. Seeing his father's situation, Daniel ensured that his son William took note, teaching him to make smart decisions that set up the family for success. Though he was a child, my grandfather William learned farming and business as soon as he was physically able. My father would say that Daniel had required William to learn how to till the land, run the businesses, and sew, all things Daniel had learned from his own father.

More Black people owned land and property in Laurel Hill during Reconstruction than they do now. As Leah Douglas commented in *The Nation*, "For a period after the Civil War, black ownership of land increased and was primarily used for farming. At one point, blacks had gained ownership over about 15 million acres, which meant that they were also in control of 14% of the farms located in the United States (that is 925,000 farms owned by black people)."[15] From the 1920s to today, the percentage of

Black landowners has steadily dropped from 14 percent to only 1.3 percent across the nation.[16]

There were many free Black communities throughout the United States prior to Emancipation. They were more common in the North, where deadly race riots erupted in the 1830s, 1840s, and 1860s, as poor white immigrants and Black American freedmen fought over jobs. Most freedmen in the South left for the Northern states or Canada. The Black Malloys felt a kinship to the land they lived on, which they saw turning into a true community. They wouldn't leave for the North until decades later.

―――

Between 1863 and 1877, Reconstruction mainly focused on rebuilding the South and supporting formerly enslaved people. In 1863 Lincoln announced his first reconstruction plan, "the ten percent plan," to diminish the Confederacy by allowing new state governments if one-tenth of voters took a loyalty oath.[17] The Reconstruction Acts made further steps starting in 1867. However, for each accomplishment toward a safer nation for all, another setback followed.

In June 1865, John Stewart Rock, a Black man, was admitted to the bar of the US Supreme Court.[18] (He is known for coining the phrase "Black is beautiful.") At the same time, the Black Codes were created in the South that guaranteed imprisonment for the slightest infraction. If a Black person displayed a bad attitude toward their employer, for example, they could be arrested and sent to prison, which was the only legal form of enslavement after the Civil War. The Black Codes were the Confederates' way of holding on to the institution of slavery.

The Freedmen's Bureau was the only ally that the Black community had. A relative of mine, another George Malloy, was a teacher for the Freedman's Bureau. Union troops were stationed in the former Confederate states, including North Carolina, to protect Black people from the increasing number of violent crimes perpetrated by white supremacist groups against them, from beatings to lynchings.

White people who were allies of the formerly enslaved, no matter their rank, were instant targets for violence at the hands of these groups. The first assassination in the history of the United States, that of Abraham Lincoln, is now described as a white supremacist crime, though that term was not coined prior to the end of enslavement. A team of societal misfits and Confederates formed at the behest of John Wilkes Booth, who attended the hanging of John Brown, plotted to kidnap President Lincoln to exchange him for the freedom of Confederate prisoners. Their plot failed. On April 14, 1865, Booth then shot Lincoln, who died the next morning. Hundreds of Black women and children stood outside all day in the rain in front of the White House, mourning his loss.

Black mourners weeping over Lincoln's death and white supremacists killing other whites proved that race was not the sole source of discord: We cared for those who cared for us, no matter their race. The constant attempts by some to thwart one group's success and position themselves higher were major catalysts for discord in that era, and they still run rampant in society today.

Another thing that angered supremacist groups was when different races joined together and looked out for one another. William was just a baby when Lincoln was assassinated, but his siblings and parents grappled with losing the president known for freeing the enslaved right after having a child born in a free country for the first time.

These events did not stop the Black residents of Laurel Hill and the Republicans at that time from pushing forward with their goals. In 1860, President Lincoln had described his own journey from laborer to the White House: "I want every man to have the chance—and I believe a black man is entitled to it—in which he can better his condition—when he may look forward and hope to be a hired laborer this year and the next, work for himself afterward, and finally to hire men to work for him! That is the true system."[19]

This sentiment was embraced by Black and white farmers, workers, and those seeking to rise from oppression in the United States and overseas. There was a new influx of immigrants from Scotland, Ireland, and the West Indies seeking the opportunity to change their lives in President Lincoln's America.

Black people worked hard on all fronts, and farms and businesses flourished. Collective political action in the community helped both Black and white Laurel Hill residents thrive, on the condition that all did their part to contribute. Thanks to laws that allowed Black men to vote if they owned land and met other prerequisites, they held high government positions. Over two thousand Black men served in political office, with hundreds of them holding local offices in the South during this time. As of 2023, we have elected only three Black governors in the history of the United States. In some ways, the world my grandfather William grew up in was more progressive than what we are experiencing today.

William would grow to become immensely proud of being a Black man. Although he would reinvest resources he gained from his access to both sides of the world back into his community, he never claimed to be anything but Black. Being Black was an honor to him. As a boy William's parents made sure their children were isolated from the mental warfare of being seen as less than.

Dr. John Kani stated in the WHUT-PBS program *Black Stage: Classical Canon* that "I'm an African and I know from my father and my grandfather and my great-grandfather that I'm a descendant of great Kings, actually I'm royalty. . . . It was preparing me against the onslaught to my humanity that would happen in an apartheid state."[20] William's knowledge of who he was and his status, community, and skill sets as a builder and entrepreneur made him less vulnerable in an unjust society—at least until his community surpassed their white supremacist neighbors in their political progress.

The Republican Party of the time was making waves supporting a progressive agenda seeking land, equal rights, and reparations for Black people in the South. During this time, the majority of Black voters were Republican. Lower Richmond County (the southern part of the county) consisted of both Black and white Republicans of that time who trusted one another, secure in the knowledge that they would vote for one another's best interests. This was before it became Scotland County in 1899.

When he was twelve, William's freedom was jeopardized by the Compromise of 1877.[21] In a dispute about the results of the 1876 presidential election, the Democrats of that time agreed to concede only if the Union troops were removed from the South. This decision left the Black community vulnerable to violent attacks and resulted in yet another increase in deaths. It was an added fear for a young Black boy after having had the protection of the Union troops.

William's childhood consisted of a myriad of triggers from the remnants of the war and Jim Crow but also accomplishments for the Black community and those seeking change in Laurel Hill and the nation. In 1877, Laurinburg was founded, and the Black residents and Republicans of that era outnumbered the Democrats and Confederates in the town. Laurinburg Republicans shifted to a focus on education, and many served on school boards and rejected laws that opposed equal education opportunities for Black children.

———

In my grandfather's community in the post–Civil War period, joy was being restored and dreams built. This was a new way of life. On land scarred by a long war, the town of Laurinburg was emerging.

A typical day in this town for my grandfather wasn't typical for other Black boys his age. Though Sundays were reserved for church, he started each morning on bended knee in his bedroom with "The Lord Is My Shepherd." A hearty breakfast awaited him, prepared by his mother or one of their workers: eggs, meat, bread, potatoes, and fruit. This set him up for a day of working on the farm planting, checking on the crops with his father, and following his every step through their acres of land.

William watched his father guide their workers, pay them, and delegate tasks. The humid summers and chilly winters affected the hours spent outside. The afternoons were for studying the Bible and math, which he was eager to learn. All Black people were eager to learn. While places like New York had Africa Free Schools for Black students founded by white abolitionists and those who practiced manumission, North Carolina was just getting started on education for Black students after the war.

The rebellion of Nat Turner, who once lived only twenty miles away from North Carolina, resulted in a law forbidding Black people in the state to read. "After the war, every former slave became a learner, every person a teacher, every place a school—or so it seemed," write Alex Sandifer and Betty Dishong Renfer. "With torn spelling books and reading primers in hand, freed people gathered in homes, in cellars, in sheds, in corners of meetinghouses, even under shade trees during breaks from working their crops."[22]

These methods satisfied William's thirst for education until physical schools were built for Black students in the community. Though the town was becoming more progressive, no one even considered integrated schools at that time.

My grandfather witnessed how a community can create something from nothing. This fueled his reach; it is vital to see people who look like you prosper so you know the possibilities and how to reach beyond. He knew of his great-uncle Dr. Archibald Malloy, a medical doctor and Union sympathizer who was shot and killed while trying to help someone with a medical concern. My grandfather William was fond of medicine and science. He dreamed of becoming a medical doctor to provide the care that was denied to Black people. But were his dreams possible for someone who looked like him? "What happens to a dream deferred?" Langston Hughes asked in 1951.[23]

3. GRANDFATHER WILLIAM

My parents ran a tight and structured ship. As a child, I often walked down the two flights of stairs in our Maryland home to find bacon, eggs, grits, toast, and link sausage waiting for me at the kitchen table. Shortly after breakfast, Mom and Dad would head downtown for their high-ranking jobs with the federal government.

My teenage brother, Leon, who was popular for his athletic prowess, drove me to school. Sometimes, he would drop me at the corner, and I would walk the rest of the way by myself. The half-mile walk felt like a marathon when I was six years old. This continued until a neighbor, Mrs. Gerstl, caught him and my father reminded him that his use of the car was contingent upon his taking me to school.

Dinner was in the dining room every night. Weekends were for choir rehearsal, Girl Scouts, camping, mother-daughter outings, shopping a few miles away at our favorite mall, or social group activities designed to give Black children opportunities to connect with their peers at events.

My mother was meticulous. Pencil-written cursive notes labeled the walls in the laundry room describing where everything needed to be placed. Sticky notes also made appearances—on the refrigerator door, on the bathroom mirrors, on the trash can, on the washer and dryer—so messiness was inexcusable. One note read, "Please wash your dishes and put them away, we do not have a maid." We were taught to show respect for our cleaning lady, Miss Hattie, who came every weekend, by gussying up prior to her arrival.

As always, church and its rituals remained a core of our lives. I recall the first pastor we met at a Presbyterian church in the DC suburb, Bob Angus, who had a family of four. His home was filled with African furniture he acquired during his missionary work.

The sculptures in his home were something I hadn't seen before. I felt connected to them. I started telling everyone I was of African descent. As a child I thought I was African with some Native American blood. I was proud. I loved the art and the culture. When my white classmates bragged about Ireland or Italy or Israel, I was happy to brag about Africa. I couldn't fathom being from anywhere else.

I never met my grandfather, but I did meet my aunts and some uncles on my father's side of the family. Both of my parents had more than ten siblings each. I met my grandfather's first daughter, Zelda, at the house of her younger sister Dorothy, while she was visiting Washington, DC. Aunt Dot was perhaps even more formal than my parents. With that Laurinburg Southern twang, she greeted us at the front door with a loud and clear "Wellsa!"—a slang fusion of "well" and "sir" that she used for her most elated greeting.

When my parents went to social meetings and events, I would stay at Aunt Dot's home. I recall wanting to join my mother at a meeting with Lena Horne, but as usual I was told, "Children are not allowed."

Aunt Zell was described as "high yellow" or a "red bone" due to her light skin tone. She could easily pass for a white woman. I would argue she was of a tan hue.

As a little girl, I thought some Black people just had white skin after seeing my relatives and knowing we were Black. This changed when a neighborhood friend was visiting. We were sitting in our living room, where an organ, a drum set, an upright piano, and a Fender Rhodes piano were part of the decor and used for both rehearsing and entertaining. As kids, we liked to discover items in the house, and that day we went looking through the leopard-print telephone table with the chair attached that my family called the booth. My friend opened a photo album and asked me, "Who are these white people?"

"Those are my aunts, my grandad, and my cousin Tootles. We are Black," I replied with a little laugh.

While looking at the photos, my friend said with the utmost confidence, "These are white people. Nobody is that light without white blood. How do you think they got that light?"

I sat on the booth and immediately called out to my mother in the kitchen about ten yards away. I pleaded for answers before I got the side eye of doom given when I dared be disrespectful.

"I thought you told me these were Black people."

"They are, but they might have some white blood in them," my mom calmly replied.

I had not yet explored or come to grips with what this exchange implied. It was a sobering thought because underneath it all, I felt there was more to the story. Maybe my parents held back because they didn't want to cause us any pain.

To me, the exquisite photos also contained stories of fear and trauma between the lines. I had to bring them out of their shelter. How sad it is to not feel okay presenting yourself as who you really are. For a child, these pictures were fun. They were family and reminded me that we were connected to many people. This felt good. But did my mother mean to tell me that we might in some way be related by blood to the people behind our trauma?

To me, this was inconceivable.

Today I understand that we are mixed people. My grandfather also had light brown skin.

Our society and most of the Black ethnicity consists of blended blood, culture, and more. The diaspora is vast and far from monolithic. How did Southern white culture and customs connect with the African culture, and how were those customs intertwined within the Black Southern culture of my father's stories of Laurinburg? His stories were so rich that the community he described sounded ideal for today, let alone the past. My grandfather William's light brown skin was not uncommon. The census, which started in 1790, helped to keep some record of whether a person was Black or mixed race. W. E. B. Du Bois stated in *Black Reconstruction in America*, "The black population at the time of the first census had risen to three quarters of a million, and there were over a million at the beginning of the nineteenth century. Before 1830, the blacks had passed the two million mark. . . . By their own reproduction, the Negroes reached 3,638,808 in 1850, and before the Civil War, stood at 4,441,830. . . . In 1860, at least 90% were born in the United States, 13% were visibly of white as well as Negro descent and actually more than one-fourth were probably of white, Indian, and Negro blood."[1]

Lighter skin was a common sight within Black communities. As genealogist Paul Heinegg says, "Most families were the descendants of white servant women who had children by slaves or free African Americans." Another factor? Many white males had children with enslaved or free Black women, and thus the Black community in the South consisted of various skin tones.[2]

Most Black children watched their families figure out how to make it and move on after slavery. If you figured out how to prosper in this time of development for the race, you could build bridges for the future generations.

As students at Howard University, my daughter and I were both told that, as Black people, we had to be better than average to get average treatment, and we had to work harder than our white counterparts. We had to show up early while others were just on time. The bar was set high due to the obstacles that existed in society.

As a boy, William and his older brother James attended Laurel Hill Church. In *The Home Place*, Nettie McCormick Henley described her experience growing up in Laurinburg as a white woman in the 1890s. She wrote, "After the emancipation of slaves, blacks continued to sit in the gallery when they attended services. Eventually, however, the churches founded by the Gaels lost most of their Black membership to their own separate Black churches. The slave gallery continued to be used by the blacks who drove the carriages for white employers, and it also sometimes functioned as a nursery for the children with the Black 'mammies' minding the young ones."[3]

In 1880, numerous Black members of the Laurel Hill Church reached out to the presbytery with the goal of beginning their own house of worship in Laurinburg, which they called Chapel Hill Church. *The Africo-American Presbyterian* shared William's experience at Chapel Hill Church as where "he first saw the light and that it will always be hallowed ground."[4] He considered that space to be sacred.

In 1883, William Malloy turned eighteen. Two years later, he received the gift of another brother, Henry Darius Malloy, who would be called by his middle name. His parents made sure William looked after him. William was happy to do so and couldn't wait to bring Darius to church with him.

William was keen on manners. Walking down Laurinburg's streets, if he passed a Gibson, a McLauren, a McNair, a McCall, a McCrae, a Stewart, a McDuffie, a McLeod, a Morrison, a Shaw, a Blue, or anyone else, he greeted them with dignity. These were some of the Black families that had Scottish names, though not all of them were descended from enslaved people. Some were given their surnames by way of marriage, birth, or inheritance.

William might stop and make eye contact and say with a smile, "Hello, how are you?" followed by a question about the person's kin or his or her day. If the discussion continued, you had to honor who was speaking; it would be an infraction of the unspoken agreement to be courteous if you cut the conversation short. The unspoken agreement about appropriate behavior was shared in all households and backed by the Bible.

How you dressed instantly announced your class. William wore only suits, a signal that he owned land and several businesses. Casual clothing such as jeans, invented in 1873, felt hats, and sack shirts were for workers and farmers. In every photo of my grandfather, he wears a suit with a gold pocket watch hanging neatly on a chain from his slacks.

In the average American household at that time, the men

supplied the income their families needed, and the women supported their husband and children by maintaining the home. In the Laurinburg Black community, in contrast, many women also worked. Though their jobs differed from those of the men, they brought money into the household. Eliza, who owned farmland, was different. She didn't work on the farms herself. She was the boss of those who did. You could stand taller when the home and the job were in order.

In our community, the elders were to be held in high regard and treated with respect at all times. "Sir" and "Ma'am" were the titles you would use for those older than you. This practice is still followed in Africa, but the titles are family related. Biko's Manna and Mfundo, a musical group made up of the children of our dear friends Ayanda and Sebone, who live in South Africa, refer to me as "Gogo Lauretta," meaning grandmother, a title conferred with high respect and given regardless of one's flaws. To them, my daughter is Aunty LeeAnét.

The village and family mentality was passed down through the generations and through travels to other countries. These traditions were embedded in Laurinburg culture and social life. Everyone looked out for the children, no matter who they belonged to, and the children followed what any elder said to them or asked of them.

———

When my father was a boy in the early twenties in Laurinburg, he was on the baseball field, mid-game, and scored his first home run. Later in the game he was hit with a bat, leaving a scar on his face outside his left eye, a scar he would keep for the rest of his life. His team lost the game. Still, the family celebrated that home run. His mother prepared a dinner with his favorite pecan pie for dessert and invited the neighbors. At dinner, William bragged about his son, just as my father did when my brother Leon scored in sports and the neighbors congratulated him. My father's celebration continued after the dinner party. When he walked about town with the family, neighbors would congratulate him on the home run.

Uplift was everything. If you opened a business, you hired from within the community. If you bought land, you sold a piece of it at a discount to a poorer family that couldn't afford to purchase it at the going price. Due to the past travesties of enslavement, there was a feeling in the air that prosperity might not last. The quickest and safest path to wealth was purchasing land and farming it so you could have something of your own. The census of 1890 indicates that members of the Malloy family, both Black and white, owned farmland.

This is how Black Wall Street communities formed and succeeded. Those who could purchase and start businesses reached back to those who couldn't.

My grandfather William wanted to follow in his uncle's footsteps and become a doctor to support his community. William did study medicine and knew how to heal, but there were too many barriers preventing him from practicing.

At the time, most white doctors who worked in hospitals would not accept Black patients. Those that did had home practices. Though you would think the Black community might have felt hindered by not being able to get treatment from white doctors, they preferred having doctors who looked like them.

Many Black doctors prior to the 1800s and during enslavement knew which herbs could heal. There were many practitioners of "slave medicine" until laws were passed to prevent Black people from practicing medicine.[5]

William would not become a doctor.

At age twenty-one, William had surpassed the skills his father had taught him. He knew how to construct a home, and he built one for himself on land in Laurinburg, ten miles distant from Laurel Hill. At the time, Laurinburg was considered a swamp; it was surrounded by water, with lower and upper regions. This natural development worked to the advantage of the Black community, as the average white person would stay away from the lower areas, thinking them less desirable. If you looked away from the muddy ground and raised your eyes, as the Black community did, you would witness the spectacular scenery of nature's gifts.

Cypress, red maple, persimmon, and majestic sweet gum trees adorned the town. An array of fish such as spotted sea trout, redfish, and spotted bass made for fruitful fishing trips. The abundant water and rich soil made for a massive harvest. Laurinburg's Black residents knew the potential of the town thanks to their agricultural skills, which dated back to Africa and Scotland. There were also a number of Native Americans in nearby Lumberton who had cultivated the land for generations, making crops such as corn, squash, peanuts, sweet potatoes, and pumpkins prominent in addition to cotton and tobacco.

The town was moving into more modern times. Main Street, while unpaved, was the central location where you could buy shoes, groceries, and whiskey. (The inebriated men at the many bars along the street made it unsafe for women to walk by alone.) The sewing machines and fabrics brought to the area by the Scottish settlers and the craft skills of the townspeople of all races meant that the quality of the clothes, shoes, and other goods in Laurinburg was unparalleled.

Due to its coastal location, the town was vulnerable to tornadoes and storms. There were as many as sixty tornadoes in North Carolina and the surrounding states in 1884 alone. The homes William built for himself and others had to be sturdy enough to withstand the torrential weather.

As a church-going man with a good job from a good family, William was well positioned to marry. For young adults, getting married, owning land, and starting a family were central to survival. At Chapel Hill, William met a woman named Minnie, five years older than him, who was to his liking. They attended church events together with family and took pirogues out on the water with friends under the serene shade of the elm trees. They had picnic lunches in the park after he met her family.

In the courting tradition of the time, you had to follow the required steps of meeting your intended's parents once you felt that a match was suitable. After you received permission, a formal engagement could be announced. Some interpretations of the King James Bible suggest that a couple must be evenly "yoked," which was interpreted to mean having similar stature in the community in addition to both being God-fearing.

Just a year after the birth of his next brother Percy, William and Minnie were engaged in 1890. The next year, William, age twenty-six, and Minnie, age thirty-one, jumped the broom. In this era, men were usually older than their wives, but in this case, William was younger than Minnie. William waited to marry until he was established and could support a wife and eventually a family. Following tradition, they consummated their relationship after the wedding.

William and Minnie lived in the home made by William's hands in Laurinburg. About three years after their marriage, Minnie became pregnant. Their son was born about 1894, and they named him William Braxton Malloy, in keeping with the German name meaning "resolute protector" and for England's William the Conqueror. William Murphy Malloy now had a son to follow in his footsteps.

It is not clear where Braxton, as he was called, was born. Given that his father knew how to facilitate a birth, it could have easily happened at home. However, I have seen a photo of the Scotland Hospital with Black people gathered in front, suggesting that this hospital did allow Black patients. (Years later, the family had to drive an hour to go to the Highsmith Hospital in Fayetteville, North Carolina, for emergencies.)

Three years after Braxton was born, the family welcomed a second son, Leland Malloy, a shortened version of the Scottish name McLelland. William now had two sons to raise and support.

Laurinburg was filled with achievers and motivators pushing the culture forward. While many community members started teaching from their homes, William took time off from the mill and his construction work to teach other Black men how to build homes. This not only helped develop the community further, adding more houses to the swampy land, but also passed on the skills of construction and carpentry.

The most popular members of the town were those who

supported others with their businesses and profits. If you owned farmland that supplied food or if you hired workers, when you walked the neighborhood, you would hear, "There goes Mister Malloy." That's how our grandfather William was formally greeted. The farmers and business owners were like local celebrities.

Though the church was central and proper manners mandatory, the Black community in Laurinburg was also ready for attack. In this little town, most people owned a rifle due to the town's proximity to the woods. Residents were armed with education, business acumen, political prowess, and ammunition.

By the 1890s, the language of the Black community was shifting with the rise in general education. Using cross-cultural phrases, they were also developing their own ways of speech. Well before Reconstruction, the Scottish residents introduced casual words such as *bonny*, *canny*, and *wee*. Not only did the Black community adopt these terms, but there were also those who spoke Gaelic. In the Malloy family, Black relatives spoke Gaelic and English. They picked up terms from both the Black community and their Scottish relatives. Scottish residents also adopted common Black terms such as *y'all*, *ain't*, and *fixin'*.

The South had, and still has, its own vernacular that wasn't Black or white: Everyone spoke the same way. You heard the same terms when at home or socializing with friends. Code-switching did occur, as you couldn't speak casually or use slang if you were Black and running for office or making a business transaction.

The language of the white residents of Laurinburg was also

shifting, depending on the area. In *The Home Place*, Henley wrote that in the late nineteenth century, her family's language "was English, with some Negro softening. . . . We used expressions that were different from those of other sections, but I think they developed here mostly—not in Scotland."[6]

The town was also fueled by customs from England. In addition to naming their children after members of the royal family, Black residents gathered for tea, dressed in the fashionable attire of London, and created social events that mirrored those of France and Europe. The Black debutante balls and cotillions date as far back as 1778; their focus was on manners and social etiquette.

In 1885 on McGirt's Bridge Road in Laurinburg, named for the longest truss bridge in North Carolina spanning the Cape Fear River, a group of Black Presbyterians started Bowers Chapel Church. George C. Carlson was the first pastor.[7] Given the new church's proximity to their house, William and Minnie joined Bowers. The church motto was "The little church that stands by the side of the road trying to do the will of God and to be a friend to man." Chapel Hill and Bowers were two of the Black-founded Presbyterian churches in Laurinburg and Richmond County.

Though the Presbyterian religion also came to the community from Scotland, when Black Presbyterian churches were founded, like Chapel Hill, they incorporated their own hymnals and music. The Malloy family loved music and singing. Though my father was no Nat King Cole, he loved raising his voice in praise. The Scottish brought snare drums, which the Black community quickly adopted, while the Black community introduced the Scots to the banjo, a staple in Scottish-Irish Appalachian music to this day. The richness and customs of the Black community included cross-cultural connections in addition to economic progress.

On the political front, the Laurinburg Republicans of the time were gaining traction and saw the opportunity to gain more power. The Populist Party focused on the interests of farmers and laborers. There were large Black populations working in these fields who were opposed to the Democrats. In order to stop the efforts of the Democrats of that time and dominate the vote, the Republicans and the Populists joined forces. This joint venture, an example of fusion politics or fusionism, helped the Republicans and Populists sweep the elections in North Carolina between 1894 and 1896, with big wins in Laurinburg and Wilmington. Reconstruction was thriving.

As a farmer, builder, Black man, and new father, William felt at home in the Republican Party of that era, as did much of the Black community. For his sons to prosper, William needed advances. In 1898, with his two young sons, one four years old and the other one year old, William was ready to vote in the next election to secure the rights of his children.

A plan was in the works to keep Richmond County as a Republican community in the Democratic state of North Carolina and to expand the progress beyond Richmond. Black enfranchised voters helped with getting Ulysses S. Grant in as president and they knew they could make a difference in the election of 1898 as well.

4. PEOPLE AND PLACES

From as far back as I can remember until I was in my early twenties, my summers consisted of escaping the suburbs of Washington, DC, to visit my mother's family in Cleveland, Ohio. My mother was the only one of her eleven brothers and sisters to leave Cleveland, where her family had settled by way of Georgia. Excursions with my cousins in the industrial city offered unlimited games with other kids my age. I felt like I had endless cousins, aunts, and uncles, as well as my grandmother, all with unique personalities.

My mother spoke distinctively, articulating clearly at all times since she was an orator and fluent in French and Spanish. She and my father pronounced my name and my daughter's name with very different intonations, as if speaking two different languages. My aunt Helen, who was a sergeant and served in the Korean War and performed at nightclubs there when off duty, had both street smarts and business acumen. She owned a brokerage company and co-owned a bar. She always said exactly what was on her mind.

My grandmother was the queen. She required all of the grandchildren to call her "Grandmother," with no exceptions and no nicknames. She was number 719 at the S. K. Wellman factory, which aided in making atomic energy and metallic friction material for brakes. She worked hard to become the owner of several homes. I remember the day she burned her mortgage papers. These are just some of the many incredible people who shaped my visits to Cleveland.

I never wanted to leave when we visited them. There was something about going to Cleveland that I couldn't quite identify. I only knew I loved exploring the various family homes with my cousins and spying on the aunts and uncles as they had adult conversations.

Ohio had abolished slavery in 1802, well before emancipation, a vast difference from North Carolina. As noted on the North Carolina Historical Sites website: "When Confederate forces fired upon Fort Sumter and President Abraham Lincoln asked for troops from North Carolina to put down the rebellion, the state acted swiftly and decisively. North Carolina seceded from the Union on May 20, 1861, and the state's involvement in the Civil War began."[1] Many Black people moved to Cleveland to escape the racism in the South and to take advantage of opportunities in industry during the Great Migration and prior.

While my mother left Ohio to attend Howard University and later to take a job in the federal government, my father left Laurinburg to fight in World War II, to attend Howard University, and then to look for better job prospects. Due to the rampant racism in the South, he found integrated Washington, DC, to be a more appealing option. As former Vice President Kamala Harris, who graduated from Howard University, said: "Our unity is our strength, and our diversity is our power. We reject the myth of 'us' vs. 'them.'"[2]

After a long visit in Cleveland, my brother Leon and I would ride in the luggage-filled Chrysler to visit Uncle Braxton, my father's oldest brother, in Massillon, Ohio. These trips to Massillon occurred until Uncle Braxton passed away when I was a teenager.

Uncle Braxton and his first wife, Dr. Viola Graves Malloy, returned to North Carolina after college. They were involved in the education system, knowing the hardships that Black students faced in the South. They were called upon to support Hillside High School in North Carolina by joining the committee to keep the school open to Black students. Uncle Braxton then moved to Ohio, where he planted roots as one of the few Black doctors in Massillon alongside his wife. After he and Viola divorced, he lived the rest of his life in Massillon with his second wife, Patience Coker, a nurse.

On our summer road trips, my parents would turn into Uncle Braxton's driveway after reluctantly listening to me sing repeated rounds of the Mountain Dew commercial. After what felt like a few miles, we would reach his home. The house was all on one level, but the driveway went longer than I could ever fully run in one try.

My father honored his siblings just as he did his own father. As the youngest, with as many as fifteen years or more between him and some of his siblings, he respected them as his elders. When the siblings gathered, they greeted each other using their names ("Good morning, Braxton," or "Good Morning, WB") and always prefaced their speech by announcing their relationship ("My dear brother . . ." or "My dear sister Fairley Mae"). To me, they were like royalty, always dressed as if going to a formal event. They regarded each other with the respect you might afford a dignitary.

While reveling in their sophisticated Southern hospitality, they also found moments of release. When Motown records spun on the Victrola, they took to the floor, each with their own unique dance style. Whether it was my father's upright camel walk and a sophisticated coffee grinder breakdance move, or Aunt Mae's finger-pointing in each direction accompanied by a facial expression with enough poise for *Vogue*, their fearless personalities shone through their every move.

As I grew older, I never grew weary of visits to Uncle Braxton and Aunt Patience's house. It was always a grand occasion stepping inside their large home, playing in the yard, and even being chased by their dog, Pansy the Pomeranian. They stayed active in the community and owned a shopping center. The laughs, the sweet tea, and the family connection took me inside the stories my father told me of Laurinburg. I traveled virtually to that town through the people and the way they connected with one another. They weren't just family, but part of a town and a county whose people made their own way.

By 1893, the residents of Laurinburg were seeing shifts in the economy and what they had access to as Black people at home and across the nation. Many mixed-race community members were excluded from inheriting the land of their white ancestors due to the one-drop rule, which saw them as Black if they had even one drop of Black blood, a fate that would later befall my great-grandfather Daniel and his mother. Though most states observed the one-drop rule, it was not law.

That year, George D. Tillman, a member of the US House of Representatives from South Carolina's Second District, opposed the legalization of the one-drop rule: "It is a scientific fact that there is not one full-blooded Caucasian on the floor of this convention," he stated. "Every member has in him a certain mixture of . . . colored blood. . . . It would be a cruel injustice and the source of endless litigation, of scandal, horror, feud, and bloodshed to undertake to annul or forbid marriage for a remote, perhaps obsolete trace of Negro blood. The doors would be open to scandal, malice, and greed."[3] He was speaking on the many ways the one-drop rule had taken a hold of the liberties of the community.

This was progress. If more states had adopted this mindset, Black people might have gained access to the land and property of their white relatives as well as voting rights and other privileges afforded to their white neighbors. The Laurinburg community was well aware of what was happening across the nation, especially in nearby communities in South Carolina.

In 1893, the telephone was just eighteen years old. Over forty-nine thousand telephones were in use in the United States,[4] but long-distance calls were very expensive, and not many people in the Black community had phones. They relied instead on other sources to find out what was happening around the area and across the nation. The Black community communicated when attending church and events where they might hear about what was happening with their neighbors. For news about people beyond their personal circle, the local newspaper was the solution. It kept them updated on political advances and allowed some relief from the day-to-day routine.

The main paper of Laurinburg was *The Laurinburg Exchange*, which prided itself on being a Democratic journal and included that word in the subtitle of every issue. It was founded in 1882 by O. L. Moore and is still published today.[5]

Issues of the paper from the nineteenth century are archived on the North Carolina Digital Heritage Center's DigitalNC website, along with other newspapers in the state. *The Laurinburg Exchange* was initially focused on sharing information on such diverse topics as the Native American community and how they survived by fishing, and happenings involving the royal family in the United Kingdom.

These early newspapers are windows into the local community from the people who lived there. *The Laurinburg Exchange* did not cover the Black community, yet local papers needed to reflect more than the white community's viewpoint. A young Black man heard the call and responded. In 1895, N. F. McEachin founded *The Laurinburg Post*, the first Black newspaper in the region, and he also served as the editor.[6] The only documented record of McEachin's life says he was born in Laurinburg in 1882, which would make him thirteen years old when he founded the paper!

A *Laurinburg Post* subscription cost seventy-five cents for one year, forty cents for six months, or twenty-five cents for four months, paid in advance. Today, that seventy-five cents would be equal to $28.28. It seems that McEachin priced the paper appropriately for his community.

The Laurinburg Post allows us to learn about the Black families and entrepreneurs who were making waves. In the few pages that were restored from the December 21, 1895, issue, we can get a glimpse of the Black community of Laurinburg.[7]

The first page featured a joy-filled poem with phrases such as "And far and near Kris Kringle's bells their airy music shake, and dancing feet of boys and girls a sweeter joyance make." Next came a Christmas story titled "As Others See Us." With hints of a modern-day soap opera, its entertaining lines include these:

"When I kissed her, she sobbed just a little and wished me good luck and whispered that she loved me. Ah, well! Those are sweet pathetic memories! Since coming to New York nearly everything I have touched has turned into gold; but I have grown rich too rapidly for my own good. But she did care for me then and I acted like a cad." The narrator continues to lament his lost love, and a spirit shows up granting him the ability to look into the future without altering it. He has an epiphany, seeing how he looks to others, and envisions his fate alone without his love.

After giving readers an escape from reality, and the editor a chance to write creatively, the paper shifted to an obituary for a popular pastor of the African Methodist Episcopal Church in Baltimore, Maryland. This is the only obituary that appears in the paper.

Later in the issue, McEachin addressed the community directly:

WE STATED SOMETIME AGO THAT WE WOULD in the near future give our readers an article along the line of progress achieved by the colored businessmen in the town of Laurinburg, N.C. We start out by saying, a bright future for the colored citizens of Laurinburg, N.C. The causes that prompt the writer to remark as above mentioned are several notably . . .

In our reference we hope no one will hold that we are egotistic. The purpose shall be to present facts, hence one of the channels referred to is the Laurinburg Post, the advent of which you know is recent. Six months ago, who of the citizens would have dreamed of a Negro journal for Laurinburg, N.C., knowing too that the depopulated incident caused by the removal of the railway shops has been so marked? But howbeit, she is here and here to stay. Why not? She is edited and managed by a

Negro, a member of that race which truly constitutes the backbone and sinew of this great South land. And I appeal most especially to my race within this county. Had this journal not a single subscriber without the county there are enough Negroes in the county to buckle down the politics thereof, and strong enough to hold up this banner journal and hold it up high and long that it may have ample opportunity to truly champion the cause of a prejudiced and oppressed people.

The relocation of the railroad shops in the decades following the Civil War was still an issue in Laurinburg because the stores had drawn tourists from other areas. In a 1916 article in *The Laurinburg Exchange* titled "Historical Sketch of Laurinburg," the writer stated, "During the Civil war the railroad moved its shops here to get away from danger of seizure by federal armies besieging Fort Fisher near Wilmington. The shops were located here under stress and fear, for temporary purposes, and there was, from the first, the instant danger of immediate removal, which hovered over this town until 1894, when the final decision took the shops away. During all these years the fear of disaster should the shops move, was so apparent that even those who were able to build largely and permanently, refused to do so."[8]

With fewer tourists and businesses, people in the town were fearful, but McEachin and the Black community noticed an upswing in Black businesses. In *The Laurinburg Post*, McEachin continued to highlight the business acumen and entrepreneurship of the Black community in then Richmond County, including that of my father's great-grandmother's family, the McNairs:

OUR JEWELER MR. CB WHO HAS BEEN a resident jeweler . . . because of his closest application to his business as well as his established efficiency as a jeweler, he has won the confidence of the entire community and enjoys the title, "goldsmith," given him by the white citizens.

No where between the "Ocean City" and the "City by the Sea" can one find the opportunity of gazing upon so fine a beef market as is kept by our enterprising butcher, Mr. Henry McNair.

Mr. Eli Roper and A. Harris are both merchants of long standing, and men who are ever at their post of duty. Mr. Roper, commonly known as "Colonel," is the only merchant that will give you 13 apples for a dozen.

Last but not least is our very own enterprising merchant and largest Negro farmer in the county of Richmond, and we would not be in error to say one of the largest Negro farmers in the state, W. P. Evans, a gentleman possessed with marked business capabilities whose every turn indicates business. In our opinion, he is truly one of the race that has substantially manifested to the world the possibility of a Negro. His success is worthy of comment.

Quite 10 years ago he arrived in this town from Wilmington, N.C., and engaged in the general merchandise business with a stock of goods possibly not exceeding $300.00 in value. He occupied a store room 16x20ft after several months of business pursuit, his business grew so that he added 16x20ft more of building, and in that he labored early and late till at last the magnitude of his business demanded more room. He effected an arrangement to purchase the privilege Roper and Harris had in a large brick building in their quarters, he was soon comfortably situated. Right here we would say that Mr. Evans success was remarkable. He not unlike other men of the race that has to contend against the superstition of his own race, along side with the prejudice that is seen on part of the whites in all communities, he has come to the front . . . today Mr. Evans occupies one of the finest glass front stores in this town. It was built in 1889 and in it he carries one of the largest stocks of dry goods, shoes, notions and groceries in the city. He also runs a gents clothing and furnishing store in a building two doors beyond his main store . . . In addition to this, he carries on an extensive wood business for two consecutive years, he has planted over 200 acres in cotton . . . Take his combined business, he gives more employment to colored laborers than all the white merchants together, besides he has befriended the race all he could . . . Colored farmers your excuse has been the reason you did not trade more with colored merchants where they did not carry what you need and besides could not furnish you to make your farm. Thank God that cannot be said longer. You have one among you in the town of Laurinburg, who has as much stock with two exceptions as any merchant in town, and sell as cheap and somethings cheaper, who is asking for your trade. He is one of your family. When a Negro businessman succeeds and thereby rises the race get the benefit of it, and when they fall the race is faulted because of the fall. This business Walter has built in our midst stands as a living monument of which Negroes can do if but the same opportunities are afforded them as is afforded the white business man . . .

Give him a trial, we guarantee that his business success will be yours and his earnings into the hands of colored young men, who will fit themselves as clerks . . . will possibly launch out into a similar business of theirs, and so on we continue to progress, and thus because we are able to support race doctors, mechanics, machinists, lawyers, ministers, and in short, all other professions in the same way as do the white race.

This is a grand and noble cause. Push it, encourage it, talk it and act accordingly, and in this way, you solve the Negro problem . . . until we build up, encourage, patronize the different business pursuits of life among the race, and do by those pursuits as do the whites by those among their race, you may as well cease discussing the race problem.

W. P. Evans, the merchant so highly praised in the newspaper, attended church with the Malloys and many others at Bowers Chapel. Bowers Chapel was one of the two Black churches listed in the paper's directory. The other was Bright Hopewell Baptist Church, further solidifying the church as a meeting place for the entire tight-knit Black community in Laurinburg. Today, the area's Presbyterian churches have no records of those who attended Bowers Chapel. The Black newspapers in North Carolina were the only ones who reported this information. The newspapers also provide a glimpse into the surrounding areas in the county. Community members from Rockingham, North Carolina, wrote to McEachin to report on local happenings.

One such report reads: "Our town is booming, and every store is filled with Christmas goods. Weddings are in abundance in this section, one and two a week."

W. G. Catus provided an update on the former Malloy family church: "The young people of Chapel Hill church raised $18.00 to pay off some long standing church debts. . . . These young people deserve much credit for their effort and so noble a cause, especially the 'Jubilee Club' with Mr. C.S. McMillan manager who rendered fine vocal music for the occasion."

The Laurinburg Post included the full Sunday sermon of Dr. Talmage, titled "Hornets Do Good: No Man Is Free from Petty Annoyances," as well as updates on national affairs. One article reports that Tennessee's chief justice David S. Snodgrass shot Colonel John R. Beasley at a law office after Beasley claimed that the justice used prejudice in a decision. Beasley was shot in the arm, and the justice was required to post bail of one thousand dollars.

The Laurinburg Post also served as a political voice. While the white Republicans were working with the Black community, they were not a monolith and some did not help the cause. After reporting on the need to support the paper and praising those who did, McEachin remarked on the members of that party who had not been aligning fully with the Black community:

> WE ARE SORRY TO NOTE THE FACT, that a Republican Judge would be the first to lead off in a thing that has always been avoided by all other Judges previous to this one. And that is sending prisoners belonging to this county to other counties to be put on the chain gang. The Solicitor whom you and I voted for, could have raised an objection to this, and in our opinion the Judge would have reversed the decision. But did he do it? Nay. This is none other than a Populist Solicitor. Had it not been for your votes, today he would be as many others, getting work to do as best he could. We trust that our Solicitor will act a little more judicious in the near future. It becometh us to note these things. We said we meant to be impartial. Tell the truth no matter who it offends.

McEachin then printed a special notice about supporting local Black businesses. He suggested going to Beecham's store for apples and all kinds of fruit, Christmas fireworks, and Christmas toys of all kinds:

> GO TO W.D. JAMES FOR FIRST CLASS millinery goods, a complete stock, besides gents, ladies and children's shoes. His salesmen are clever and polite. You have only to try and be convinced of the fact that you save 10cts on the dollar, by going elsewhere you lose it. W.P. Evans sells the prettiest fitting ladies' shoes in town. Don't delay, go at once and get a pair. The cash store is the only house in town selling granulated sugar at 5cts a pound. You can get your Xmas goods cheap by going to R.E. Lee's. The cash store has a complete stock of both staple and fancy goods.

He also published a detailed national report on cotton sales.

Henry McNair, an ancestor of my father's, placed an ad in the paper for his store and restaurant. He noted that "beef pork and pork sausages, fish and oysters and such other edibles are usually kept in first class market cheaper than what you can buy elsewhere in town. Also, I have arranged a department in which I am selling apples, oranges, candies, bananas, coconuts, chestnuts, peanuts etcetera cheaper than any other dealer. A first-class restaurant in the rear of my market meals at all hours, oyster stews on short notice I am yours to please Henry McNair North Carolina."

Maybe this is why oyster stew was one of my father's favorite meals. I remember how he made it for me using milk, butter, salt, and pepper—simple ingredients, but rich in flavor.

On a torn and ripped page of *The Laurinburg Post* there is a clear advertisement for W. P. Evans's shoes. A button-up leather boot with a slender look was on sale for $3. A drawing of a white man appears across the boot. In fact, everyone pictured in the paper was white. This could be a result of the prevalence of the white gaze, which many Black writers from W. E. B Du Bois to James Baldwin to Toni Morrison have addressed. In a 2017 NPR article titled "Writing Past the White Gaze as a Black Author," L. J. Alonge defines the white gaze as "the assumption that the reader is white and the resulting self-consciousness in your thinking and writing."[9]

Though *The Laurinburg Post* was written for the Black community, it contained statements aimed directly at white Republicans. It's also possible that the photos were part of an effort to gain customers of all races, given that goods in the shops owned by Black merchants were more competitively priced.

The last page of *The Post* focused on the spread of catarrh, a condition that was more common in those parts, and contained many ads for tonics and potions claiming to cure catarrh as well as other common ailments of the time, including chronic dyspepsia, nervous fits, and eczema.

As far as crimes in Laurinburg, the paper reported this story:

> THOMPSON WHITE HAD A HEARING before Esquire J. P. McRae, Monday, charged with having entered the house of Mr. August, McKinnon and after making several cursing threats of what he intended to do to Mrs. McKinnon and he (Thompson) seized a chair and had it not been for some of the colored folks on the place, who came to Mrs. McKinnon's rescue, this scout of a white man would have no doubt seriously injured her. When on the witness stand denied knowing anything at all about his actions . . . He was required to give bond for his appearance at the next Superior Court and upon failure was sent to jail. Truly it can

be said of Mr. McKinnon that he is an exceptionally good man, and one who strictly respects the laws of the land, else would have certainly made it only to warm for Thompson. Your motive to let justice be meted out to this transgressor was a righteous one and only shows what kind of material lives in this community.

McEachin replied to this story and another, "Ain't those two cases a clear demonstration of the fact that the citizens in this town and community will not resort to lawlessness. We love to comment on the goodness of a people. We hope that the day will never come to Laurinburg and the people of her community when we have an occasion to reverse our condemnation. To do the right thing to a right cause and at the right time, is the characteristic of this people."

The issue ended with a few additional ads for local businesses. But one standout item was a note on how to behave: "*The Post* will not appear next week. The next issue (D.V.) will appear on Jan. 11th '96. A merry Christmas to all. We trust that none of the readers of the *Post* will be guilty of spending their holiday in rioting, but of a sober temperament."

The Post carefully documented how the local Black community in Laurinburg was adding layers of character, culture, and civic identity: taking a political stance, encouraging the support of Black businesses by Black community members, featuring writing by both women and men, and reporting on national news tied into the goals of the larger community.

The Laurinburg Post did not last many more years, though there's no record of the exact date of the final issue. McEachin died in 1900,[10] perhaps as a result of what happened at that time in Laurinburg.

5. A BACKYARD WAR

In 1898, William, Minnie, their four-year-old son Braxton, and their two-year-old son Leland were making do in the county of Richmond. Married now for seven years, William was becoming the family man of his dreams. His construction company was gaining a small reputation, and his family had a humble home in Laurinburg.

William wanted his sons to live out the dreams he himself had been denied. He started to set aside funds for his children to attend college. Meharry Medical College, Hampton Training School for Nurses, Howard University, and various hospitals for Black people provided opportunities for them to study and have careers in medicine.

His family was spread throughout the city. William's parents, Daniel and Eliza, did not live near William in lower Richmond County. The houses in Laurel Hill where Daniel and Eliza lived were much larger than those in Laurinburg. William was busy with building and setting up his family; he didn't have a lot of time to visit his parents. His white uncles, Daniel's half-brothers, lived on that side of town, and some of them were Confederates.

At the time, white Republicans were working with the Black community to help farmers, strengthen the economy, and improve the schools in the area. Many of the white children worked on farms, while the Black children focused on education. For the formerly enslaved, sending their children to school filled them with a new sense of pride. The schools were well supported.

In Richmond County, school funding was determined by the number of enrollments; since the Black schools had more students, they received more funding. The white upper class wanted no part of lower Richmond, where whites and Blacks were creating a new society.

In Richmond County, the Black community was focused on education for the next generation as well as farming and the economy. Both white and Black Republicans and fusionists shared these interests and saw the benefit of addressing these needs.

In 1893, 35 percent of white children were in school compared to 60 percent of Black children. In most years, Black schools received an equal amount of funding, if not more than white schools, and the majority of Black residents also owned farmland.

The lower percentage of white students in school was in part a result of six mills opening in the area, forcing poor white adults and children into low-wage labor and sharecropping alongside Black people in order to survive.

Daniel M. Jackson, a Black man, was elected to the school board, which was required to have an equal number of Black and white members. The Republicans and fusionists also created new amendments to election mandates calling for equitable voting policies.

William saw Black schools thriving. A better education and future lay ahead for Braxton and Leland once they were of age.

William also knew that growing his business would give his children additional money and opportunities. He grew up working with his father and learning from him, and in turn, he wanted his sons to have the option of running his construction company when the time came. He also knew the benefit of having his sons manage the company and work as teenagers.

Oliver Dockery, an ally for Black people in Laurinburg and the surrounding area, formed the Reconstruction government with freedmen in Richmond, with a base in Rockingham. According to the press, Rockingham had an unusually large number of white Republican residents. Dockery was known for not fully supporting the Confederacy during the Civil War, which was frowned upon in a cotton-driven community. After the war he quickly shifted to supporting Reconstruction efforts and got other white people to join him. In a printed ad created by the early Democrats, Dockery and his supporters were surrounded by drawings of blackface minstrels.

The Fusion Party was the original name for the Republican party in many states. The name itself sprang from the consolidation of many parties, including some Democrats who opposed slavery. With these leaders in place, the white supremacist focus of the state government started to spill into Laurinburg. Many today may find the alignment of the two major parties to be diametrically opposed to where they stood in the post–Civil War years on issues such as states' rights and racial equality.

Thanks to the efforts of Dockery and Republican and fusionist candidates working with the Black community, hundreds of Black citizens in town were becoming registered voters. Newly registered William was one. He was eager to see the changes designed to aid Black farmers. In 1894 and 1896, the Republicans and a fusion party composed of Republicans and members of the

Populist Party collaborated to defeat the Democrats. The word was spreading on the voting power of the Black community. "The Black man whose voting power had merely been lying dormant, reappeared as a potent political force," wrote scholar and historian H. Leon Prather Sr. in *The Journal of Negro History*.[1] While other states disenfranchised Black voters, more than 150,000 Black voters were registered in North Carolina.[2]

With white Republican allies in Rockingham, Williamson, Laurel Hill, Stewartsville, and Spring Hill, Black residents joined forces and thwarted the efforts of Democrats to create Scotland County, which would separate Black and white Republicans and fusionists and allow Democrats to rule. They had been successful at avoiding this separation for thirty years.

Though North Carolina as a state was ruled by Democrats and had new voting policies that allowed Black men to register to vote, Democrats couldn't penetrate Richmond County for years.

Educating the Black community and having them join forces with white Republicans of varied economic status was stirring the waters: Richmond was a threat to the efforts of Democrats and the Confederate community to maintain control.

A similar alliance of white allies and Black people was forming in Wilmington, North Carolina. In 1898, Alexander Manly, the owner of *The Wilmington Daily Record*, the only African American newspaper in that city, caused a stir with his response to an attack on consensual biracial relationships by Senator Rebecca Felton, an avowed feminist and slave owner. In a speech, she declared that Black males were raping white women and needed to be suppressed. Manly, who was mixed-race himself, responded by stating that Black men were not rapists and that white women were encouraging their advances. Many were fearful about challenging a US senator and putting another spotlight on Wilmington.

Black businesses such as laundromats, tailor shops, and independent schools were popping up in town. In 1880, Richmond County was 50 percent Black; by 1890, it was 54 percent Black.

In the shadows lurked white supremacists, and each achievement in Richmond added more fuel to their fire. Every effort they made to dismantle the coalition of Republicans and Black people was thwarted.

Daniel Russell was elected governor of North Carolina in 1896, the first Republican since Reconstruction to hold that office. Russell often worked in alignment with Senator Jeter Pritchard, a fusionist leader.

The Democrats in town started paying attention to other Democrats in places such as Halifax County, where residents and politicians were making violent and aggressive moves against the Black population. Wearing red to symbolize blood, the Red Shirts were one of the earliest white supremacist groups in the United States, organized in 1875 to oppose Reconstruction. They were a more organized version of the rifle clubs that proliferated in the Carolinas after federal forces broke up the Ku Klux Klan in 1871.

It was rare to see Democratic leaders donning red shirts, but they always attended rallies, pushing efforts to sway the public by force if they deemed it necessary. The Red Shirts were not the only supremacist group involved; there were also the Rough Riders, comprised of veterans from the Spanish-American conflict.[3]

The railroad in Laurinburg allowed the wealthy to travel and support businesses in other locations more easily. Ahead of the

1898 elections, white supremacist rallies focused their hatred on Black and white Republicans and fusionists. If you were caught supporting the Black community, the Red Shirts and supremacist groups might say you were "blacked" and therefore ought to be handled without regard to your race.

White supremacists in Laurinburg—fueled by anger at the Black community's advances, collaboration between Black and white people, and a lack of jobs for working-class whites—provided the Democratic Party with a launchpad for many rowdy rallies, the first of which occurred in the spring of 1898.

Before the first riot, knowing that the Red Shirts were becoming active, Governor Russell reached out to the federal government to ask for assistance from US marshals to help keep the peace and protect all citizens from potential havoc. Whites were arming themselves, and Black citizens were purchasing weapons as well.[4]

Senator Pritchard, a Confederate veteran, also wrote to President William McKinley asking for protection. The press leaked the story, which made Pritchard shift his stance. Local politicians wanted to prove that Laurinburg could manage on its own. In the end, the federal government did not send help.

As the sun set in Laurinburg, North Carolina, on May 30, Memorial Day, a sea of Red Shirts descended on the town. "When Democrats kicked off the state white supremacy rally in Laurinburg in 1898, they chose neither date nor place at random," historian Gael Graham wrote. This would give enough time to affect the election, and Laurinburg was pushing against changes that white supremacist groups wanted to make in education, the separation of the counties, and the unity of the fusionist party. Two thousand people showed up, most wearing red shirts made of calico, flannel, and silk representing the blood they vowed to wade in if necessary. Their shirts were made by their wives, who also prepared their meals. Their pants were tucked into their boots.[5]

In *The Home Place*, Nettie McCormick Henley wrote, "Dr. Kenneth Blue was a leader of the Red Shirts in Laurinburg, and the white men in and around Laurinburg rallied around him, all dressed in red shirts and black pants firing 'Little Zeb.'"[6] Little Zeb was the name given to the cannon in the community named after Governor Zebulon Vance, known for his conservative stance and racist language. The cannon sat on display in the local courthouse well into the twentieth century. She also wrote about how some white Republicans who supported the Red Shirts came up with ways to protect their Black workers: "We believed the Red Shirts were necessary, and it was a protection to our Negroes for Frank to be a member."[7] Frank was a member of her family.

The supremacist groups traveled on horses, buggies, and carriages bearing Winchester rifles, shotguns, and pistols: a festival of sorts steamrolling into the small town. Torches flared as the sun grew dimmer and the procession continued. The red shirts, the flames, and the horses' hooves beating into the dirt roads struck terror in the Black residents.

Candidates for political office were also present, dressed in the typical suits of the period. Their attire distanced them from those who were there as "muscle." Speeches from Democratic gubernatorial candidate Charles B. Aycock and others rallied the crowd, which grew to thousands. Talk of Negro domination and the need for white supremacy in Richmond County elicited a roar of approval from those assembled.

And then violence broke out. "They had parades to scare white Populists and the Negroes," Henley wrote, "and when some of the ringleaders would not scare, a bunch of the Red Shirts took them out and beat them and ran off."[8] Graham noted,

"Mobs shot into the homes of black and white Republicans and populists and a black church but reserved physical violence for African Americans. Black residents were pulled from their homes and whipped and beat and murdered."[9]

In November 1898, Wilmington's *Morning Star* reported, "The white men of Richmond County showed their determination. . . . It showed that the white men do not propose to longer endure the domination of the black race in this section."[10]

Taught to protect women and children, William secured his home from the troop of two thousand supremacists that flooded Laurinburg. The Black Malloy men bore guns and knew how to use them. William saw his fellow Black landowners, farmers, workers, councilmen, and members of the board of education run for safety.

Acting quickly, he took Braxton to his father's house in Laurel Hill, where he would spend the remainder of his childhood. At one point after the rally, William was forced to leave the area with Minnie and Leland. Their first girl, Zelda, was born around this time, though we don't know her birth month amid the chaos.

The Morning Star also detailed a speech at the rally by Claude Kitchin of Halifax County, who would later run for congressman, who "appealed to the people of Richmond County to follow in the wake of Halifax, where if a negro constable came to a white man with a warrant in his hand he left with a bullet in his brain. His review of the scandal and extravagance of the Fusion administration was very forcible, and, in fact, his whole two hours' talk elicited vehement applause. Mr. Maxcy L. John presided at the meeting."[11] Kitchin was based in Scotland Neck, part of Halifax County, another town named for its Scottish immigrants that had a large Black population. Located by the Roanoke River, the farms thrived, and the landscape looked like a paradise. It was another area they sought to remove Black residents from.

Many Black voters left Laurinburg after the riot, and some did not return. Their safety had been compromised and there was no sign that this would change. Others held on to their community, as they sacrificed too much to build their homes and town to desert it. One could not judge the former as there were more opportunities and growing economies for Black people in the North.

Efforts to intimidate voters were not limited to these rallies. Merchants threatened to halt selling food and products to those who voted Republican or fusionist, and lives were threatened. The rallies continued throughout the state along the Black Belt, areas with a Black majority known for their high-yielding crops. As stated on the Black Farmers' Network website: "America's Black Belt Region has been historically known for its plantation lifestyles and overt acts of racism."[12]

The rioters marched to New Bern, Fayetteville, Concord, Roxboro, Reidsville, and more to hold their rallies. In each location, Charles Aycock led the fanfare, showing up like a preacher leading a flock. Sometimes the Red Shirts wore all white, and sometimes they turned the torture festivals into barbecues with as many as 142 lambs and pigs roasted on site.

"Thousands of cheering white women waved flags and handkerchiefs as a long column of armed and menacing men rode by," wrote Prather. "On November 1, 1898, Laurinburg Red Shirts of Maxton, Laurel Hill and Gibson showed up four hundred strong with a mile long procession."[13] The message was clear: The Democrats of the 1800s would win the election peacefully, if possible, and violently, if necessary.

The Morning Star noted that over five hundred Black people in Richmond removed their names from voter rolls ahead of the election: "Many negroes have taken their names from the registration list. From November 8th the white men will rule Richmond County."[14] On Election Day, white supremacists armed themselves and turned up at the polls, which were devoid of Black voters. We don't know if William was able to vote, as only a few Republican and fusionist votes were tallied.

When Governor Russell returned to Laurinburg after voting in Wilmington, he was met by a mob of supremacists who vowed to inflict harm. He hid in his buggy for the day—humiliating for a public figure of his stature. Although the Democrats swept the elections, the rallies were not over.

On November 10, two days after the election, the mobs converged on Wilmington, North Carolina, known for its fusionist and biracial community and political leaders. With the support of Democrats in other cities, including Laurinburg, the mob infiltrated Wilmington, the streets, the businesses, government offices, and more, perpetrating the worst violence up to that time. It was a coup d'état, the only known violent takeover of a government in the history of the United States.

Various white supremacist groups stormed in by train, on horses, and in buggies. It was a premeditated event, organized and supplied by people from many states. Gatling guns were provided, as were rifles, cannons, and torches. Black homes and businesses were burned down. More than sixty people were reported murdered, but the true number was probably greater. The office of *The Daily Record*, the prominent Black newspaper whose editor had challenged Senator Rebecca Felton's charge that Black men were rapists, was also burned down.

The local government was overthrown, and entire towns were destroyed. The post–Civil War healing was reversed by beatings, murders, and other forms of violence. While Democrats and white supremacists in Laurinburg bragged about what they saw as victories, the Black community supported those whose homes were destroyed in the Wilmington massacre. In Richmond, Republican leaders such as Walter P. Evans took in his Wilmington relatives.

In 1899, the Democrats successfully separated Black and white Republicans by creating Scotland County out of the parts of Richmond County with the largest Black populations. This separation of the Black community from its white allies and from the white supremacists pleased the Democrats.

It also allowed the Democrats to have better control of the town of Laurinburg, removing funding without harming anyone outside the Black community. William and Minnie witnessed a war in their own backyard. Blood had spilled years before during the Civil War. William relied on stories to envision that war, but this one happened right before his eyes.

Just as his father had witnessed slavery and the Civil War, my grandfather witnessed an attack on his freedom and his community. He saw his neighbors being attacked for participating in democracy, but it seemed that many did not fight back. Although some Black residents owned guns, there were no reported injuries or deaths of members of the supremacist groups in Laurinburg.

Though Democrats of that time had won the election, the supremacist groups still continued their rampage. In Richmond County, Duncan McPhatter, a Black man, was lynched by an angry mob. By 1899, all Black school board members had been removed, and the next year Charles Aycock was elected governor of North Carolina.

The white press reported the massacre in Wilmington as a race riot caused by Black people, and this remained the narrative for decades. (When we spoke with a friend who was born and raised in Wilmington, she told us she didn't learn of the massacre until well into her sixties.) On November 11, 1898, *The News and Observer* in Raleigh reported: "Negroes precipitate conflict by firing on the whites. . . . Building of . . . slanderous paper gutted and burned. . . . Eleven Negroes were killed. Three whites wounded. . . . City under control of new and conservative democratic government. Mayor Waddell puts guards around jail to protect Negro prisoners."[15] Earlier that week, *The Morning Star* in Wilmington had reported, "White men were forced to take up arms for the preservation of law and order."[16]

The laws that Reconstruction Republicans had put in place were overturned, including one that required an equal number of Black and white members on the school board. Only seven people in Richmond rejected the overturning of this law, and only two in Wilmington.

Starting in 1899, new laws were passed to maintain the Democratic Party's white supremacist power structure permanently. On January 6, 1899, Lieutenant Governor Francis Winston, a former Republican turned Democrat, introduced a suffrage bill to keep Black people from voting, a disenfranchisement amendment made to block the US Constitution, which granted Black people the right to vote. It included a poll tax and a literacy requirement.

Since there were also many illiterate white people, he added a grandfather clause that extended the franchise to those with an ancestor or relative who could vote before 1867.[17] After the government takeover, racial hierarchy laws and extreme segregation laws upheld in the landmark Supreme Court case *Plessy v. Ferguson*, such as those prohibiting Blacks and whites from sitting together in public, further separated and halted relationships between Black people and their white allies.

The number of Black children in school dropped from 87 percent before the insurrection to 65 percent in 1904 after school funding decreased. The new county schools designated for Black students were poorly supported and became among the worst in the state.[18] The public school system founded by the supremacist groups would remain in place for the next eighty years.

Black communities throughout North Carolina had been ravished. With the creation of Scotland County, Richmond was severed. What would the Black community in Laurinburg do to recover, to restore, to rebuild?

William had a newborn girl and two young sons. The trauma from the attacks had put a strain on his marriage. For strength, the community drew on the religion that their oppressors assumed would keep them in their place. But their African roots were infused with secret codes; when they prayed and sang the songs of their ancestors, they were reminded of what they had overcome and of their ability to escape, as well as their power to heal mentally, physically, and spiritually. Accustomed to moving through trauma, they called on their faith, their education, and their history to create a strategy for moving forward.

In the years of Reconstruction, Black people in what became Scotland County bought land and started businesses. Walter P.

Evans, an elder in the Presbyterian Church and a member of the same fraternal order as my uncle Emmett, was originally from Wilmington and owned a popular mercantile store on Main Street in Laurinburg. The store opened in 1884 and had customers of both races. Known as an active Republican, Evans was targeted by an angry mob after the massacre. They surrounded his house and called him out. Luckily, a doctor said he was sick on his deathbed with pneumonia, causing them to leave.[19]

Knowing that change had to start with education and safe Black schools, Evans concocted a plan. In 1904, the Tuskegee Normal and Industrial Institute was all the buzz as a prosperous Black college. Evans reached out to its founder, Booker T. Washington, as well as William J. Edwards of Snow Hill Normal and Industrial Institute, a Black school in Alabama with as many as four hundred students. Evans envisioned a private institution focused on trade and education for Black students. Washington sanctioned a new school, and Evans called on Emmanuel McDuffie, a former Snow Hill student, and his wife, Tinny, for assistance. They moved to town to start Laurinburg Normal and Industrial Institute.

William had land and his construction company. This was his weapon against any barriers that he had ready when needed. After the Institute was officially founded in 1904, William was ready to send Braxton, age ten; Leland, age seven; and Zelda, age five or six, to the school.

Four years after the school was founded, Minnie suddenly passed away at age forty-seven. Now William was a widower with three school-age children.

6. POST-INSURRECTION

As a child, I loved our Saturday afternoon drives from the suburbs of Maryland to Newton Place in Northwest Washington, DC. In the 1960s, sitting in the back seat of my father's blue Pontiac felt more like riding in a boat than a car. Driving down Georgia Avenue, I watched the view shift from tree-lined roads and dirt paths with the occasional rabbit or deer to storefront businesses, restaurants, and clusters of row houses with identical stoops and porches.

As an inquisitive, rambunctious, yet well-mannered five-year-old child, I was eager to see my beloved Aunt Dot, who had helped raise my father. She was my parents' go-to babysitter in the summer. In the back seat, all I could think about was eating her homemade biscuits, which were crisp outside and soft inside and tasted perfect.

During the fifteen-minute drive to DC, my father planned the family meeting as he drove and my mother watched the road and worked crossword puzzles. At age fifteen, my brother, Leon, had his transistor radio to his ear while plotting how to get a biscuit from Aunt Dot's refrigerator before the meal.

Once I was inside Aunt Dot's row house on Newton Place, which was pristine and clean with everything shining, including the plastic on the couches, I made my way to the most exquisite homemade biscuits on the planet. I would hear her belt out, "Ask first if you want something from the kitchen, okay?"

I was always on my best behavior at Aunt Dot's and followed her house rules. I always showed the utmost respect for my elders, and I appreciated that she believed I could exhibit such self-control as a kid. I was allowed among adult company if I stayed still.

Though Aunt Dot never had any children, visits to her house often included a child or friends she looked out for, like my childhood friend Tonowa, who was often visiting her cousin four houses down. This was also where Uncle William's (Grace's husband) cousin Thurgood Marshall visited. To this day the family speaks about him being our cousin with pride. I also saw Aunt Dot's husband, my uncle Oliver Robinson, and my big cousin Tootles, pronounced "Tooles" by the family.

After brunch, I sat quietly on the living room couch, knowing not to say a word while my father pulled out the tin box and placed it on the hand-carved wooden dining room table. Once he flipped it open, we knew the meeting was about to begin.

The tin box held a cascade of files and handwritten papers related to what my father said was one hundred years of land ownership. Lined up at the table as if at an executive board meeting were Dot and Oliver, Grace, Fairley Mae (or Mae) and her husband Dave, their sister Odessa (or Dess), Uncle Smitty, and my mother, Loncie. At that family table sat entrepreneurs, business owners, teachers, and federal government workers. Before the fictional George Jefferson made waves on television, Uncle Smitty owned a series of laundromats, which made him a superhero to me. He always humored me when I questioned him in make-believe meetings as I mimicked my father in the most serious way possible.

I sat on that couch in silence as the adults talked business, and the conversation became more intense. My father made sure that the family's land and estate in North Carolina stayed up to date. He would discuss whether a property was to be sold or whether there were taxes to be paid. In addition, as the executor of the estate, he collected rent from the properties the family owned and distributed it among the family. It was a proud moment for the family, but I didn't really know why Dad was so very serious and stern. If even a piece of paper in his handwritten ledger was ripped or missing, he would yell out his favorite phrase: "Loncie, help!"

It was important to maintain our affairs in Laurinburg and retain what my grandfather had built. The meetings were always productive, never failing to get through the itinerary. They not only made sure the land and legacy were secure; they also kept the family connected, given that some members lived in different states.

Change came in 1968, as the riots after the assassination of Martin Luther King Jr. made traveling down Georgia Avenue in Northwest Washington, DC, unsafe. My father was leery of taking us to what felt like my second home in DC. The neighborhood shifted from peaceful and well-kept to uneasy, with boarded windows on every other business. I became concerned for our family and our Laurinburg estate meetings. It's hard for a community to recover after collective trauma on both a surface level and a systemic level.

After the collective trauma of 1898—the torture spree, the Wilmington massacre, and the change in government—the Malloys were also dealing with grief, as 1898 marked the death of William's father, Daniel Murdock Malloy, in his early fifties.

There is no record citing an official cause of death, but we suspect he was killed in the rallies that took place in the Black communities (also referred to as the Black hamlets) that year. The truth of his death was buried with him at Patterson Memorial Cemetery in Laurel Hill, which holds many secrets. Eliza, then a widow, remained in their home in Laurel Hill where Braxton was raised.

President William McKinley was well aware of what was occurring in the aftermath of the insurrection, as detailed in *Teddy and Booker T.* by Brian Kilmeade:

> IN THE DAYS AFTER THE WILMINGTON MASSACRE, [Booker T.] Washington got wind of President McKinley's plan to come to Atlanta for that city's peace jubilee. The educator hurried to Washington [DC] to ask the president in person to visit Tuskegee while he was in the region. He told McKinley that the events at Wilmington and elsewhere—the massacre in North Carolina was hardly an isolated incident—had left "the colored people greatly depressed."
>
> The president was sympathetic: "I could perceive his heart was greatly burdened," Washington observed. McKinley accepted the invitation of the man people had begun to call "the Wizard of Tuskegee."
>
> The president arrived on December 1, 1898, accompanied

by Mrs. McKinley, much of his cabinet, several of the commanding generals from the Cuba expedition, and the governor of Alabama. The distinguished visitors were greeted by the entire town, Black and White. . . . Washington had also carefully choreographed a parade involving floats that displayed the work of the institute's many departments in agricultural and industrial training. . . . After escorting the visitors to Tuskegee's new chapel, Washington told them how honored he was at their presence—but he didn't lose sight of his purpose.[1]

Washington then addressed the president and other dignitaries by stating, "We welcome you all to this spot, where without racial bitterness, but with sympathy and friendship, with the aid of the state, with the aid of black men and white men, with southern help and northern help, we are trying to assist the nation in working out one of the greatest problems ever given to men to solve."[2] The word was out about the trials in Laurinburg but the damage had already been done, and the local government overturned.

Many Black residents had left Laurinburg. According to my father, William left Laurinburg only once, around the time of the coup d'état. The thought of what he experienced scared me. My father would say, "He left, but he came back, though!" Why would he leave, I wondered? Was he neglecting his family responsibilities? Did someone intimidate him? My father never specified if he took Minnie, his first wife, and the children with him. Knowing Minnie was pregnant, we assume they all fled for safety. I found some documents placing them in another town around that time. They returned home when the rallies were over and the mayor of Wilmington assured them that they could go back. The town would be safe unless he wanted a better job over a white man or wanted fair wages and working conditions. These were life-or-death choices. In 1899, a man named Sam Hose was threatened with death for wanting to take time off to care for a relative.

White supremacy was not only an attack on the physical well-being of Black people; it was also mental and spiritual warfare. How could a group of people become so inoculated and have such malice that even their children were accustomed to watching lynchings, mutilations, and other brutalities? The Black community knew not to challenge supremacist groups unless they liked the festive parties where "strange fruit," as Billie Holiday described lynchings, hung from the poplar trees and were viewed with delight. The rallies that took place were similar to the picnics that took place at lynchings during slavery.

There were at least 130 lynchings in North Carolina, including in Richmond County and Scotland County, between 1865 and 1946, according to the website A Red Record, which documents lynching sites in the South in honor of the work of journalist, activist, and researcher Ida B. Wells-Barnett.[3] The lynchings in Laurinburg were rare. There were some people in the white community who believed that the lynchings performed by supremacist groups showed poor character.[4] The victims included anyone who aligned with the Black race.

Many in the Black community, including the Malloys, followed the Bible and believed Romans 6:23: "For the wages of sin is death." This scripture stopped many in the Black community from seeking direct revenge because they believed that those who caused harm would be punished by God.

In my studies at Howard University, I specialized in substance abuse, suicide, and therapy. Several studies showed that guilt and shame occur when you know you caused or took part in the serious harm of others. The body recognizes exposure to abuse and abusing others as a threat to its emotional state and tries to protect itself. This wears down the immune system, which also supports people physiologically. I think back then that people must have known that there are mental repercussions to harming others. It's a type of Newton's Law: For every action, there is an equal and opposite reaction. It all balances out naturally, just as a farm can resolve any problem if set up in the proper natural order: If the insects are eating the fruit, the birds will eat the insects. Life has a way of naturally resolving matters—or at least, it should.

In 1903, more than two thousand Black Carolinians came to Laurinburg for a Fourth of July celebration that focused on hope and solidarity in the face of tactics used to destroy their accomplishments.[5] They didn't show up with guns, though they owned them; the goal was to respond with solidarity and community to the turmoil they had suffered. This was a signal to the supremacist groups as well as inspiration to push forward.

———

Education would fuel that forward motion. In 1900, the public school system spent $7,390 on white schools and $4,849 on Black schools, with $4.01 spent on each white student versus $1.46 on each Black student.

In 1896, the numbers were different. That year, $4,484 was spent on white schools and $5,381 on Black schools, with $1.47 spent on each white student and $1.62 on each Black student. Many of the white students were from working-class families and worked on the farm or in the factories; they had not previously been denied an education like Black students.

Fast-forward to 1904 when Laurinburg Normal and Industrial Institute was founded. It had just a few students, one building, and little money. Meanwhile, the government spent $7,313 on white schools and $2,168 on Black schools, with $7.98 on each white student and $1.31 on each Black student, the most drastic difference in spending the county had ever seen.[6] There was a new government in Scotland County led by Hector McLean, who was regarded as the founder of the county, and Maxcy L. John, the first superintendent after the coup d'état.

The Democratic Party at that time failed not only Black residents but also poor whites who had supported the supremacists. With no child labor laws in place, the mills of Scotland County were staffed by many white children who were not in school and had to contribute to their households.

The inequality in school funding led to the establishment of private Black schools like the Institute that stood independent from the local government. In addition to offering what today is known as core curriculum courses such as math and English, Laurinburg Institute also taught blacksmithing, laundering, dressmaking, printing, and other practical work skills. The curriculum connected directly with the views of Booker T. Washington, who stated, "Political activity alone cannot make a man free. Back of the ballot, he must have property, industry, skill, economy, intelligence, and character."[7]

Laurinburg Institute was the first Black boarding school in the United States and the first that catered to grade-school students. It followed the name and style of Tuskegee Normal and Industrial Institute—which was funded by Black and white donors in Alabama, run by Booker T. Washington, and known for being home to the revolutionary scientist George Washington Carver—and Snow Hill Normal and Industrial Institute, founded by a Tuskegee graduate.

It was controversial to mix labor-based courses with core studies, as many in the white community felt that teaching core curricula would place Black workers above their white counterparts and would halt the supply of cheap labor for the wealthy, while many in the Black community wanted to remove work-based training altogether. Booker T. Washington felt both were valuable because they offered students more options and opportunities. The work of a poet, he believed, did not outweigh the work of a blacksmith.

In 1905, a man named Frank Shaw also opened an independent school. His school was located on his property and enrolled only a small number of students, but the word was spreading.[8] The community made sure everyone was cared for, no matter what their financial situation. My cousin Wilbur Malloy, who grew up in Laurinburg, recalled, "Frank Shaw and my grandfather had a little farm store and allowed people to come and pay as they went or what they could pay later if in need."

In 1908, with Minnie now deceased and three children to raise, William needed to rebuild his family. Now in his early forties, he sought a new mate. A woman of that age would have been considered old, but he was still a young man. With an active construction business and land of his own, he was seen as a good catch. Just as he was strategic with his business planning, he had to choose a mate who aligned with his status and needs.

Like many Laurinburg residents, Annie Morton had Native American bloodlines. Currently Scotland County has the third-largest number of Native Americans in North Carolina at 14 percent. Annie's mother, Fannie, walked the Trail of Tears, participating in the forced displacement of over sixty thousand Indigenous people in the United States.[9] Fannie, who worked as an upholsterer, was listed on the Dawes Rolls, the report of individuals accepted as members of the five Indigenous tribes to be given homestead property. Annie's father was Emmanuel Morton. We don't know his occupation, but we do know that Annie was the eldest of six sisters.

Annie dedicated her time to the church. She worked with the Sunday school and taught Bible lessons. Months after Minnie's death, William began to court Annie after meeting her at church.

In 1909, William and Annie said their vows in the Laurinburg Presbyterian Church. Annie was in her late twenties, while William was over forty. This age difference wasn't uncommon: Annie's mother was thirteen years younger than her father. William fell in love with her passion for church and children, and the connection between them grew strong. He was also well aware that she was still young enough to have children, and he wanted to expand his family as much as possible.

William was on a mission to raise children who would contribute to the betterment of the community culture. He wanted to pass down to his sons both his construction business and his love of medicine. He was a follower of Booker T. Washington's theory of focusing on voting and loading yourself with skills and knowledge. All of his children were put in school with the goal of the boys becoming doctors and the girls attending college to become nurses or teachers.

Also in 1909, Booker T. Washington came to town to speak about education, the new institute, and the next steps for Laurinburg's Black community. His speaking engagement gave hope to an audience that included Black and white residents. This integrated turnout was yet another sign that the community was regaining the synergy it once had.

Shortly after their marriage, Annie became pregnant with her first child. Later in 1909, she welcomed another boy into the family. He was named Emmett, a German name meaning "truth."

In the next two years, they had two more children: Dorothy and Fairley Mae. With William Braxton, Leland, Zelda, Emmett, Dorothy, and Fairley Mae, my grandfather William was now the proud father of six. Using his skills as a builder, he expanded their home and built new houses as needed on the property he already owned.

Around 1905, the storm of Jim Crow was spreading across the area and surrounding the newly founded Scotland County. The massacre, rallies, and election were the perfect breeding ground for this period of upheaval of progress. Jim Crow, which came to refer to laws that enforced racial segregation, was taken from a blackface minstrel character created by white New Yorker Thomas D. Rice. Frederick Douglass described this caricature—and those who performed it—as "filthy scum."[10]

The coupling of Jim Crow laws with disenfranchisement, discussed in many studies in the years following the Wilmington massacre, began to dash hopes for rebuilding integrated communities. Merriam-Webster defines *disenfranchise* as "to deprive of a franchise, of a legal right, or of some privilege or immunity, especially to deprive of the right to vote." The word that sticks out in that definition, in addition to *vote*, is *privilege*, a term often used in connection with the white race.

Disenfranchisement not only stripped Black community members of the right to vote; it also took away other legal rights and created barriers for those who wanted to run for positions in government at any level or to maintain previously elected roles. It broke up communities by splitting counties and rewarding those who switched sides after supporting Reconstruction efforts. It reversed access and created systemic blocks to the reparations and privileges that had been promised by removing resources from the newly separated areas that were not majority Black.

The races had been getting along well enough until more Black people started owning farms, making livable wages, starting businesses, hiring more employees, gaining positions in the government, and outperforming some of their white counterparts. Whites who were unemployed or living in poverty made up the majority of the supremacists who turned to violence. The wealthy supremacists did not get their hands dirty.

Did this mean that the hatred that turned into torture rallies and a massacre stemmed from the economy versus overt racism? In any case, the new changes in government and society reignited an obsession with hierarchy and abuse based on the construct of race.

Now the town was separated by more than just the new county: Jim Crow also created geographic separations. The Wilmington, Charlotte and Rutherford Railroad had run through Laurinburg since 1861. The only existing photo of the Red Shirts who led the massacre and riots was taken at the train station in Laurinburg. The shops in the station had been burned down in 1865 by Union soldiers and were later moved. The train mostly carried fruits, such as cantaloupe and watermelon. Now the route shifted to the Wagram-Raeford line, built in 1909 by the Aberdeen and Rockfish Railroad, which ran between Johns and

East Laurinburg.[11] The railroad was a large factor in the town's economy until the development of the textile mills.

As in many towns, there was a clear line of segregation. Some communities were separated by hills, with the Black residents at the bottom, and others were divided by bridges. In Cleveland, my relatives shared stories about not being allowed to cross the bridge to the "white" side of town, which was the West Side during that era. The railroad tracks became that marker in Laurinburg. Black business owners with any wealth were able to cross the tracks, like Walter P. Evans, who owned the White Front Department Store on Main Street, a general store with a mail-order shoe department and a large white clientele, and W. A. Neely, who owned a blacksmith business.

In a photo taken in 1910 of W. A. Neely's blacksmith shop, white people and Black people stand together as patrons. Standing and sitting in buggies on a dirt road in front of the large wood building, the women wear colonial dresses while the men wear three-piece suits made of the finest materials. Every dress and accessory displayed their status. In 1910, there were still numerous Black farmers who owned more than fifteen million acres of farmland; this number would decrease to less than six million by 1969.[12]

William could also cross the tracks without being questioned or harassed. His construction and fabric businesses were valuable to the Black community and the white community alike. Having access to the other side of the tracks wasn't ideal for everyone. As the Black community was rebuilding, so was the culture. With laundry stores, blacksmiths, private schools, construction businesses, churches, and more, all Black-owned, there weren't many reasons to cross the tracks to begin with. The implication that Black people were not wanted on the "white" side of town and faced danger there added to their decision to stay on their side of the tracks.

Laurinburg Institute started to gain traction in these years, with more students and funding, especially after Booker T. Washington's visit to town. However, the roads and other infrastructure were not tended to. They were receiving fewer resources well before the first instances of redlining.

What happened when you had a white parent or white relatives and you were not allowed on their side of town because you were considered Black due to the one-drop rule? This question affected Braxton, who spent a lot of his time and often stayed with his grandparents Daniel and Eliza on the other side of town.

Unafraid, William took trips where he deemed it necessary. He could at times pass solely due to his skin tone, though he never pretended to be any race but Black. With his children, it was a different matter, as they all had different skin tones. As Jim Crow caused more separation and forced people to pick a race, some Black people chose to be white if they could pass.

Jim Crow was built on the invention of Blackness, a construct that originated in the 1400s during the Portuguese colonial period. The first people enslaved at that time had white skin, and the slave drivers could not easily identify them when they escaped. So they shifted to darker-skinned people, whom they labeled Black, by traveling to Africa and capturing, kidnapping, and using other methods to enslave them. The South African History Online website notes, "The Portuguese encouraged wars between rival kingdoms to maintain a constant supply of slaves. The result of this was that the region was constantly at war and millions of young people, mainly men, were forced to leave Africa."[13] Prior to this, there was no such thing as Black or white.

More labels came after as the races mixed with each other. As scholar F. James Davis writes:

> THE TERM "MULATTO" WAS ORIGINALLY USED TO mean the offspring of a "pure African Negro" and a "pure white." Although the root meaning of mulatto, in Spanish, is "hybrid," "mulatto" came to include the children of unions between whites and so-called "mixed Negroes."
>
> For example, Booker T. Washington and Frederick Douglass, with slave mothers and white fathers, were referred to as mulattoes. To whatever extent their mothers were part white, these men were more than half white. Douglass was evidently part Indigenous as well, and he looked it. Washington had reddish hair and gray eyes.
>
> At the time of the American Revolution, many of the founding fathers had some very light-skinned slaves, including some who appeared to be white. The term "colored" seemed for a time to refer only to mulattoes, especially lighter ones, but later it became a euphemism for darker Negroes, even including unmixed blacks. Given widespread racial mixing, "Negro" came to mean any slave or descendant of a slave, no matter how mixed.
>
> Eventually in the United States, the terms mulatto, colored, Negro, black, and African American all came to mean people with any African ancestry, while the terms Black, Negro, African American, and colored include both mulattoes and unmixed blacks.[14]

During the Jim Crow period, white-owned restaurants, restrooms, and water fountains were labeled with signs that read "No Negroes" and at times "No Jews" or "No Mexicans."

LAURETTA MALLOY NOBLE AND LEEANÉT NOBLE

———

For thirty years, Laurinburg residents coexisted with their white allies and created new paths forward. With leaders such as Booker T. Washington and the major newspapers paying attention to Scotland County and Laurinburg, the community's time to soar had arrived.

In 1916, Braxton, age twenty-two, was gearing up for Meharry Medical College, Leland was in college and working with his father in the construction business now known as W. M. Malloy and Son; and Zelda, Emmett, Dot, and Fairley Mae were attending Laurinburg Institute. With six children in school and on "righteous paths" and a dedicated wife who feared God and loved the church, life was looking good for William. This was also the year Annie became pregnant with her fourth child and the seventh in William's growing family.

7. ANOTHER NEW BEGINNING

As a young Black woman and a fashion major at Howard University, I viewed the world as completely open and limitless. I charged toward anything I desired, wanting to absorb all I could. I took breaks from school to get married at nineteen and have my daughter at twenty, then went back to Howard more than once, switching my major from fashion to acting to voice to music therapy as my goals and interests changed.

I will never forget the devastated look on my mother's face when, in the early 1980s, the afternoon before spring break, she found out she wasn't going to be the next pastor at our church. My mother felt her rejection was a type of discrimination, and it hurt her soul. She had put in years of work in the church, teaching Sunday school, directing the cherub choir, and serving as the interim pastor to the liking of everyone. Many spoke of her uplifting sermons and the hymns she sang, including her favorites, "Ride on, King Jesus" and "If I Can Help Somebody."

The congregation raved about her powerful soprano voice, which rang through the sanctuary. The community loved her, and most considered her a dear friend in whom they could confide.

As I recall, her supporters included Mrs. Naomi Waddleton and many more from the community, as well as her Alpha Wives sisters, most of whom said Loncie was their best friend.

In the seventies, female pastors were far and few between due to traditions in doctrine. It wouldn't be until decades later that our church would have its first female pastor. My mother was usually a beacon of joy, even when trials were afoot, but that afternoon, I could see instantly that she was forlorn. Not getting hired as pastor wouldn't stop her from moving forward with her divinity calling, but as she sat in the living room with her head down, saying, "I can't believe they did this," I knew the hurt would linger.

My father was very strict when it came to protecting the women in the family. My male friends, including close male cousins, were not allowed upstairs in our home unless they were spending the night. If they were upstairs to stay over, my father would be on watch to make sure no boys were in the girls' rooms, not even to play a board game or watch television.

He would yell out, "No men upstairs!"

I would reply, "It's a cousin!"

And he would reply, "I don't care who he is. If he's a *he*, he can't go upstairs."

My first real date was with Owen Duncan. We were both around fifteen years old. Shirley Duncan, his mother, was a popular piano teacher. She and my mother were close friends and often sang together and were hired soloists at local churches. My parents knew Shirley and her husband well.

Though societal standards did not favor women, my father supported my mother and, in his booming voice, bragged about every dream and goal she achieved. In the same way that he was a walking résumé for himself, he informed all who knew him that my mother was a published children's author whose books included *The Wedding of Butternut Kisses and Fresco the Great* and *A Gift for the Whole Family*, which I illustrated for Vantage Press. My mother worked with the likes of Russell Woollen (National Symphony Orchestra), Paul Robeson, and Dizzy Gillespie, and performed at Carnegie Hall.

He campaigned for her to become the pastor of our church and complained to anyone with ears when she didn't get the role. Though he bragged about my mother, I often wondered what *his* dreams were. Did he have some beyond what he had realized?

At parties my father would stand up and speak louder than most to make a speech that was infused with a joke: "Thank you for coming today. We were glad to have you. I made sure to get my hair done. You know, in all my years, I have never dyed my hair." Then he would pause and smile and make eye contact with a few people in the room before he went on: "I don't dye my hair. My hairdresser does!" Riding on the laughter from joke one, he would add another classic: "I still have all my teeth, these are mine, I bought them!" After the laughter died down, he would instruct the partygoers to enter the living room or dining room, depending on the plan. His character filled the space, and he made sure he was seen and heard and spread joy.

Though my mother was a singer and artist who traveled to New York and recorded three albums (*Love? Love! Love!!*; *When Your Baby Loves You, You Holler Don't Stop*; and *Soulful Songs of Inspiration*), she also taught music lessons along with managing the household. If my father had any dreams that went beyond what he did for a living, he didn't share. The unspoken rule was that men stuck to what was considered a practical job that would guarantee an income and provide for the family.

He put away his trombone as a child and hoped I would stay

away from the entertainment field. Though my mother worked, he let her know she didn't have to. He would often tell me and LeeAnét the same: "You all don't have to work; I'll take care of you." My mother wanted to make her own money and to have her own agency beyond being a wife.

Throughout my life, my father spoke of the women who raised him, the matriarchs of his family. His mother, Annie, bore some resemblance to my mother. I think of her as Miss Ann, since that's what my aunts and uncles used to call her because she was stepmother to some of them. I didn't know who they were talking about at first. When Aunt Dot, Aunt Grace, Aunt Mae, and my father would gather at Aunt Dot's house, they would giggle if someone acted too bougie. For example, if Mae came down the stairs five minutes late for dinner or if she committed even a slight infraction of tradition, they would say, "Okay now, Miss Ann, thank you for that grand entrance." And they would say it with a Southern twang and attitude, with their noses turned up and a slight shrug of the shoulder.

It was sarcasm at its finest, which was interesting for me to watch and maybe one of the reasons I was very quiet in my youth. I also knew I would be shushed quickly if I spoke out of turn. My relatives were as entertaining as the eclectic characters on the North Carolina–based sitcom *The Andy Griffith Show*, my father's favorite television program.

In his 1895 "Atlanta Compromise" speech, Booker T. Washington said, "It is at the bottom of life we must begin and not the top. Nor should we permit our grievances to overshadow our opportunities."[1] Washington's focus on education at all levels, including craft work, wasn't universally applauded in the Black community. Shomari Wills wrote in *Black Fortunes*, "In 1905 W. E. B. Du Bois . . . organized a summit of black leaders. . . . More than two dozen attendees huddled together and laid out a plan for a movement that countered the overtly conciliatory politics of Booker T. Washington with a call for farm ownership, good jobs, and self-defense from lynching."[2]

The building of Black communities was not limited to Laurinburg. Thanks to an oil boom in Oklahoma, by 1905 the Greenwood district in Tulsa consisted of multiracial workers and wealthy Black entrepreneurs, such as millionaire Ottaway W. Gurley and John the Baptist Stradford, who purchased land to develop a booming Black district. They held opposing views, with Gurley following Booker T. Washington and Stradford following W. E. B. Du Bois. Washington and Du Bois both wanted the best for Black people in America, but their approaches differed.

In 1913, Washington followed the pattern that began with Laurinburg Institute of sanctioning schools for grade school education within the Black community. As stated in a National Park Service lesson plan by historian Rebekah Dobrasko: "Public schools in the South were racially segregated in the early 20th century. The school boards generally gave more money to support white schools than black schools. The Rosenwald school building program gave African American communities funding to build and supply schools for black students between 1913 and 1932."[3]

According to an article in *The Laurinburg Exchange*, the Rosenwald program came about as a direct result of Washington bringing the idea to Julius Rosenwald, who was the president of Sears, Roebuck and Company. The schools were funded with Sears, Roebuck money and built in a number of Southern states. "North Carolina had the most [Rosenwald schools] of the southern states at around 800," writes Jael Pembrick. Further, the program "stimulated the building of more than 5,000 schools, vocational workshops, and teachers' homes in the South."[4] The article lists the schools that were in or near Scotland County during these years. They included Laurel Hill School located near the Old Carver School, Louisville School, Baysville School, Chapel Hill School near Old Laurel Hill Church, Matthew's Chapel School, Palmer's Memorial Church School, Cool Springs School, Hasty School, and another school in the Laurel Hill area for which the name is currently unknown.

In addition to the schools, Laurinburg was making other needed improvements. In 1914, Main Street was paved and overhauled from a scene likened to the Wild, Wild West in the late 1800s. Instead of thirteen bars, now both Black and white people owned independent businesses on the street. The paved road offered quicker access from Main Street to the homes, and fewer horse apples dotted the road.

Laurinburg's Black residents admired Booker T. Washington for his work with the Tuskegee Institute and Laurinburg Institute, his visits to the town, and his Christian faith. When Washington passed away on November 14, 1915, after a long struggle with malignant hypertension, he left behind a tremendous legacy.[5] Both Black and white citizens in Laurinburg mourned him. They were able to honor his legacy through the Institute and continued focus on education. William and Annie were determined for education to remain a central part of their growing family.

In 1916, Annie was pregnant again. Still, she had to tend to the five youngest children, from five-year-old Fairley Mae to twenty-year-old Leland. Unmarried children, unless in school, remained at home—another unwritten yet strictly followed rule. The eldest child, Braxton, was at Meharry Medical College in Nashville, Tennessee, the first medical school for Black people in the South.

The founding of this school harkened back to Laurinburg's history of Scottish immigrants. In the early 1800s, the wagon of a Scottish-Irish immigrant delivering salt fell off the side of the road one rainy night. The driver trudged through the stormy weather, ending on the doorstep of a recently freed Black family. They took him in and cared for him, then got his wagon out of the ditch.

Samuel Meharry vowed to do something for the Black race. Years later he and his brothers gave thirty thousand dollars to start a medical division dedicated to Black physicians at Central Tennessee College. In 1915, thirty-nine years after its founding, Meharry received its own charter. Braxton was at this newly chartered school with other young Black physicians-to-be.

Starting in 1866, Tennessee enacted twenty Jim Crow laws. Once Braxton stepped outside the walls of Meharry, he was relegated to segregated train cars, streetcars, and more. Those who violated the law were forced to pay a hefty fine of as much as $25 (equivalent to $724 today) for each offense. At least within the walls of Meharry, Braxton could focus on his studies rather than worry about basic survival.

In 1916, William hired workers to assist with the farm. They tilled the acres that extended behind the Malloy home and planted corn and cantaloupe, a fruit that thrived on Laurinburg farms. The town became known as the cantaloupe capital, a title Laurinburg gave itself because of the large number of cantaloupes exported across the South.

At home, a helper aided Annie with preparing food, cleaning the house, and getting the children ready for school. In addition, Annie trained her girls in how to run the house, teaching them how to prepare breakfast and clean. There was an order to the way women operated in the home, just as there was in the manner William trained his sons to work for W. M. Malloy and Son.

Annie gave birth to her third girl, Grace, in 1916. The baby's name reflected Annie's deep connection to God and the church. Zelda, the eldest girl, helped care for Dot and Mae, while Dot and Mae looked out for Grace, and Leland helped with the family business.

W. M. Malloy and Son was prospering. With Leland's focus on carpentry, which he studied at Laurinburg Institute, he and William built sturdy homes. If a family was small, they built a one-room bungalow. If the family was larger and had a bigger budget, they would shift from wood-frame construction to brick. The front area of the houses they built let everyone know the family's status: A larger porch, columns, and other frills gave the clear message that the family was well-off.

In 1916, most homes did not have indoor plumbing or electricity. However, some of the houses William built did have electricity, while others had posts for candles throughout. Advances in construction from 1916 to 1920 allowed the company to make homes more quickly with new materials, including metals, cement, and filler, which explains why some homes built in 1920 have lasted for years. William was meticulous, making sure that every house he built was well put together and designed to withstand storms and hurricanes. The homes in the community had their own Southern flair.

An auction announcement about one of the houses built by W. M. Malloy and Son in *The Laurinburg Exchange* in 1918 read:

Left to right: Fairley Mae Malloy standing at a distance holding a bow, and Dorothy Malloy leaning on the target as they study archery while attending the Barber-Scotia College summer learning program. *Courtesy of the Presbyterian Historical Society, Philadelphia, PA.*

June 1970. My mother, Loncie, was the Cherub Choir director at Northwood Presbyterian Church. I am third from the right, sitting on my knees.

Summer of 1983. Having a blast with the family in Cleveland, Ohio, my cousin Donna Marie Butler and I laughed so hard we toppled over on everybody trying to pose for the picture. My daughter, LeeAnét, is being embraced as the youngest in the arms of my mother. *Row 1*: LeeAnét, Loncie; *row 2*: Donna Marie Butler, Prunella Kinds; *row 3*: me (in yellow stripes), Myrtle Butler, Elsie Whitfield, Helen Norwood; *row 4*: William "Bill" Norwood, Ralph Norwood, Robert "Bob" Norwood.

1963, Ames Street, Washington, DC. My big brother watching me from a distance with his hat on after I took off running to play with the girlfriends on the block, and they squeezed my cheeks.

My only first cousin, Tootles, the first grandchild of the William and Annie tribe, on his wedding day with his wife, Bernadine Solomon Thomas.

1951. Here the family is dressed in fine threads in anticipation of Aunt Dot's fresh Southern biscuits and holiday meal made from scratch. Deacon Robinson, also a Mason, who was fondly known as Uncle Oliver to us, sits at the head of the table prepared to set off a flurry of tears from Aunt Dot and Aunt Grace with his blessing of the food and the people in the room. He was a powerful orator. Tootles smiles in front in his new tie; Aunt Grace poses with her hand on her knee; my mother, Loncie, is to the right with my brother, Larry "Leon," on her lap; my father, Lawrence, grins next to her; across the table a cousin leans in; and Aunt Dot shines her smile behind Tootles.

1955. *Left to right:* The McLaurins from Laurinburg, Dizzy Gillespie, Mommy with Larry "Leon" on her lap, and her best friend Mrs. Wall behind her gather for a photo on the sofa in our first house on Ames Street in Washington, DC.

Here is Uncle Emmett, who I thought was Daddy's twin. He just kind of disappeared one day and I never really knew why, but I found this picture of him from his yearbook when he was attending Johnson C. Smith University while preparing for a career in dentistry. *Courtesy of Johnson C. Smith University.*

1971. Headed out with the family, most of whom were Daughters of the Eastern Star. *Left to right:* Aunt Mae, who would announce her own arrival to the camera my father flashed in her face, "Mae from New York City"; my father, Lawrence, in one of his flashy bow ties; my mother, Loncie, in the middle; Aunt Dot and Aunt Grace looking hip for a night out.

Our Queen of Cleveland, Helena Dixon Norwood Haley, who only let us call her Grandmother, nothing more or nothing less, and who was a staunch supporter and campaigner for Carl Stokes, sits in the center with my mother behind her and Aunt Helen (a.k.a. Sergeant Norwood) on her left. Grandmother worked hard. I will never forget when she paid off her house, which was passed down in the family and built wealth for generations of her offspring.

I got the opportunity to get this shot of one of Grandfather William Malloy's houses, the one he built for Aunt Odessa. It burned down one year after this picture was taken in Laurinburg in 2017.

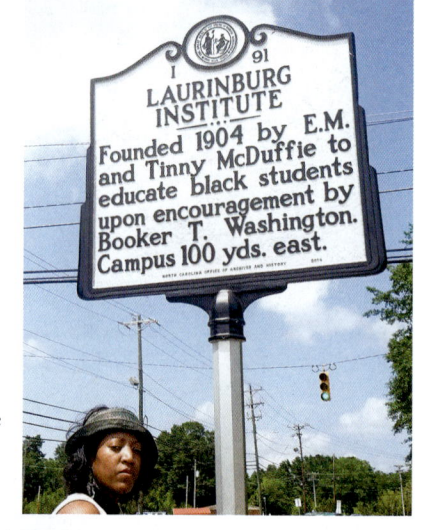

LeeAnét posing in front of the Laurinburg Institute marker. No matter the current state of the town, it still holds an incredible history that we will forever honor in our lineage.

Left to right: Grandma Malloy, Hattie Shaw, and her daughters standing proud in Laurinburg, possibly in the mid-1930s. They lived in a separate home. The other half of the family and my grandfather would travel back and forth. This was his third and last wife. He was proud and bragged about finding a wife that he was so fond of this late in his life.

The Malloys were the only family who had a car in town during my father's early years in Laurinburg, and they always dressed in suits. Here he is with one of his Cadillacs, the only brand he drove. He loved to match his suit color to the car color and often had a big hat. This might be why my daughter and I are also known for donning hats.

Here is my father, Lawrence, sitting in his office as the postmaster at Howard University. Howard University was where he met my mother in the 1940s, where my daughter and I attended, and where he worked for decades after graduating.

At age ninety-six, Dad was always ever so happy to get a hug. This photo, taken by my daughter, LeeAnét, is now the only photo I have of the two of us in his later years.

One of my mother's album covers with Russell Woollen of the National Symphony Orchestra.

During a visit from family friend Dizzy Gillespie from the Laurinburg Institute, Loncie sings while he plays the piano. They also performed in New York together.

Daddy wrote books about his life to share with all who lent an ear. Here is the cover of one focused on my mother and him.

We love to see Laurinburg, North Carolina, revived after storms and other issues. They are bringing back the factories, bringing back the jobs. Here I am on the historic Main Street.

LeeAnét poses in front of the Stewart-Hawley-Malloy House. This house was built in 1790 by Scottish immigrant James Stewart and was later owned by General Joseph Hawley, who supported anti-slavery views and worked to give plantations to freedmen. Due to his views on freedmen, he was forced out of the South in 1837. The house would later shift to Harry Malloy, a relative of Charles Malloy. It is the oldest house in Scotland County and carries a rich history. General Sherman's army made their way past this house.

LeeAnét poses with the family name. It was our surprise to recognize how much we were part of the town, deep down inside, and we felt it once we set foot in Laurinburg.

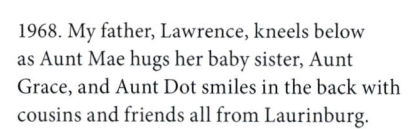

1968. My father, Lawrence, kneels below as Aunt Mae hugs her baby sister, Aunt Grace, and Aunt Dot smiles in the back with cousins and friends all from Laurinburg.

January 1, 1910, McNeely's Blacksmith in Laurinburg, North Carolina. Through the haze of the photo, you can see three-piece suits and top hats as the men pose by their horse-drawn carriages in front of this Black-owned business. *Courtesy of the Collection of the Smithsonian National Museum of African American History and Culture, Gift of James M. Baxter.*

1950s. My father, Lawrence, enjoying time in Cleveland getting to know Loncie's family, which included twins, my cousins Elsie Whitfield and Alicia Warren (previously Norwood).

740 Newton Place, where my parents, Loncie and Lawrence, met and were married. "Stand right there and don't move," my father told my mother when they met, and it seems like they got married in that same spot.

Charter members of the Massillon Urban League as featured in the *Evening Independent* newspaper on May 13, 1954. *Standing left to right*: League President Henry H. Grant and Dr. Oscar Ritchie. *Seated left to right*: Mrs. C. L. Albrecht, James Wood, and Dr. William B. Malloy. *Courtesy of the Massillon Museum.*

Regal in all photos, Hattie Shaw and William Murphy Malloy on their property, where they had workers and hired hands for their farm and house. They always gave back and supported the community.

My big brother, Larry "Leon," was a star athlete who won many awards. He was also one of the few Black students in our suburban Maryland community. Here he is soaring in the long jump competition in high school.

Remy Gee standing in front of the Malloy/Jordan East Winston Heritage Center (Forsyth County Public Library) in Winston-Salem, North Carolina. LeeAnét shared the story of Laurinburg and the Malloy doctors with her acting student Remy Gee in Washington, DC. Remy traveled to the library dedicated to the family.

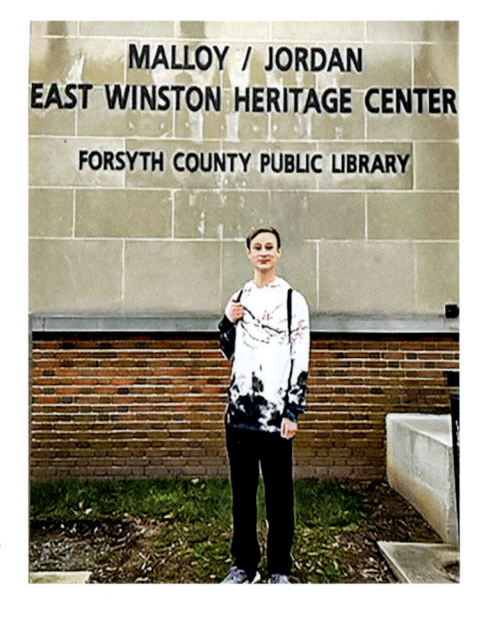

THE DR. W. T. HERNDON RESIDENCE on Conly street in the Town of Laurinburg will be sold at auction. TUESDAY, NOVEMBER 19th. . . . . This 9-room modern home is located in a most desirable section of Laurinburg—good neighbors and close-in. A little more than a block from Main street. On north side of Conly street, opposite the First Baptist church and adjoining the lots of Dr. Peter McLean and Mr. G. W. Goodwyn. A commodious home with all modern conveniences, 6 closets, bath room, pantry, electric lights, water and sewerage. Lot fronts 65 feet on Conly street and extends 150 feet to alley. Has good barn and cook house, with running water in barn. Remember the date—[6]

If a family was in need, a plan was worked out so the family could pay over time for their new home. Leland would collect the payments in addition to working on the homes. Together, William and Leland helped with building and repairing structures that were damaged in storms. William would eventually gift Dot and Grace, once they were of age, individual houses the company had built.

Annie set the schedule for the house in the same meticulous manner she used to run her church groups, writing out the chores and schedules for the children and the workers. Like others in the community, Annie faced pressure to make sure everyone could see her doing her part. Too much was at risk: The more you had, the more you were expected to give, in whatever way you could. Annie led activities in the church and assisted others in need in addition to tithing. Given that William was the builder of the church, as his wife she was a vital part of the congregation and a mother figure to many.

Physical appearance was as important as acting dignified and giving back. Annie and William dressed in the finest of cashmere. The men wore suits with vests made of satin or wool and creased pants with open pleats. Today my forebears would be ready for the fashion runway.

But however fancy their dress, their ego and demeanor had to be humble. They walked tall with dignity, but through their hard work in the community and at their job, they showed that they did not think they were better than anyone else in town. Annie came from a family that worked hard. Coming from a family that pushed hard may have been what drew her to William, as it is probable that she had more than one suitor.

While Annie ran studies, functions, clubs, and more at the church, William gathered with other local men to help govern their part of town. At these informal meetings, which were held at a house or at the church, local business owners and other prominent figures balanced mint juleps, tea cakes and cookies, and laughter with cigars and strategies to stay in tune with one another. They would discuss how to support Laurinburg Institute and made regular donations. They kept tabs on local white supremacist activity and ensured that everyone's job was secure or their business was in the black. If that wasn't the case, the discussion focused on ways to support local businesses by becoming a patron or raising money at a church service.

In 1916, car and truck ownership in the United States increased by one million from the previous year. The Malloys owned a car that was similar to a Ford Model T. Depending on what they needed, the family might put a day aside to travel to Main Street for shopping or to the home of a neighbor who might have the supplies they needed at hand. Main Street was only 1.4 miles away but the activities took the day.

Driving to town was a big production. They had to put gas in the car the day before, as there were few pump stations nearby. The workers had to be instructed to keep a close eye on the house. Clothes were set out, and food was packed. Not having enough gas or being underprepared for a trip into town could have dire consequences for a Black family. They couldn't take any chances with young children in tow. If there was an upcoming church event, everyone in the house supported Annie's efforts for weeks in advance.

Holiday parties, trips to the stores for clothes or supplies, a picnic in the park, a fishing trip, birthday parties, church events, visiting neighbors or family, and attending Sunday service were all considered special occasions. It took days or weeks to prepare and schedule for them. In the Malloy household, each event was festive and had the grandiosity of a royal soiree.

Annie's average day began when the rooster crowed at five in the morning. Emmett, Dot, and Fairley Mae followed the path set by their grandfather Daniel and prayed on their knees at the edge of their beds, giving thanks to start the day. The girls had their own room and the boys had theirs, up the flight of wooden stairs. These prayers were personal yet said out loud, so that their parents heard they were lifting their voices to God, as in church.

As the eldest girl, Zelda went from her prayers to assist Annie with baby Grace, while the children of age continued to get ready for the day. After bathing Grace in the basin and putting her in a flour sack, Zelda and Annie made breakfast. By 6:30, everyone was bathed and dressed, and made their way to the kitchen table. They showed affection in the standard Southern way, with what we call a "church hug"—not too tight and not too close. A kiss on the cheek accompanied the greeting as each child entered the kitchen to get their plate.

Although safe and sound at home, the family conducted themselves with many safety checks throughout the day. Most everyone in the Black communities knew one another or were related, all the way from Wilmington to Chapel Hill to Fayetteville in North Carolina, to Cheraw and other parts of South Carolina. William conducted business in many of these areas. When a Malloy traveled to another area, they might be asked their name if they weren't recognized. This was common practice. The practice of saying hello, asking for a name, and having a conversation was not just a show of hospitality: It was also for protection and assistance in the event that someone went missing.

Letters or notes were sent ahead of time describing who would be coming that way and why they were coming, even if it was just to pick up supplies, so that other members of the community could keep an eye out for them.

William would leave his home office at the same time every morning. Around ten, he inspected his home for upkeep, made sure the workers knew their assignments and duties, and made sure his sons were close by unless they'd left for school.

He also had to attend to medical matters. Any members of the Black community who knew medicine were on community call, as if at a hospital. His employees and workers were his family or friends or just folks who needed a job. During the day, William might eat a packed lunch of dates, egg salad, and peanuts in the shell. He would return home around six, by which time dinner would be ready.

After saying a grace that could be a service in itself, the family would break bread and then discuss their next steps. Sewing, studies, and saying the Lord's Prayer would be the children's assignments before going to bed. William would then spend some time reading books or newspapers such as *The New York Age* and *The Laurinburg Exchange* or writing letters to his brother and mother. This was before daylight saving time was introduced. After a few hours of these activities, it was time for prayers and bed.

In a town dedicated to farms and crops, including cotton, the weather held ultimate power over the economy. A drought or rainfall was big news. In 1918, the Fourth of July edition of *The Laurinburg Exchange* reported, "Very thankful for a generous rain, which fell here yesterday afternoon, the first real season we have had in three weeks; and corn gardens, cantaloupes, etc., were suffering considerably, while cotton seemed to hold its own and worry little over the drought."[7]

Crops were of interest to everyone. There were nearly one million Black farmers across the United States by 1920, and they owned the equivalent of $326 billion worth of land today. Farming was a profitable business that provided for Black families. The Malloys kept farms in addition to their other businesses well before sustainable living was a trend.

Statewide, Jim Crow laws were still being rolled out, attacking education and more. They included mandates such as this: "Books shall not be interchangeable between the white and colored schools but shall continue to be used by the race first using them."[8] Per Peter Bean in an article for the Wilson Center: "North Carolina began heavily zoning and prosecuting people for moving out of their residential zones as early as 1911. African Americans were confined to certain parts of the cities."⁹ Members of the Black community had to be vigilant about learning the new laws as they were announced to avoid being arrested or fined.

Many Black men in the community, like Walter P. Evans, who were politically involved and wanted to change the status of Black people joined Prince Hall Freemasonry, a branch of North American Freemasonry for African Americans. Booker T. Washington and W. E. B. Du Bois were members, as were leaders in a new wave of Black thinkers. Later, Emmett Malloy and Dizzy Gillespie joined.

Today's members of the order, which was founded by abolitionist Prince Hall in 1784, still fight for racial and social justice as well as equal, fair, and dignified treatment for Black citizens. As with any fraternal society, the Freemasons hold the details of their efforts and bylaws in extreme confidence.

The National Association for the Advancement of Colored People (NAACP) was founded in 1909, the year Annie and William were married. In its seventh year, Du Bois was the only Black man on the executive team. In 1917, the NAACP opened its first branch in North Carolina, focusing on anti-lynching efforts, tending to the needs of the Black people in the state, and offering legal assistance in cases of illegal discrimination and violent crimes against people of color.

Though segregation bred higher crimes against Black people, it also gave rise to new white allies: "The NAACP's founding members included white progressives Mary White Ovington, Henry Moskowitz, William English Walling and Oswald Garrison Villard, along with such African Americans as W. E. B. Du Bois, Archibald Grimke and Mary Church Terrell."[10] Other white allies attended speaking events led by Booker T. Washington in Laurinburg.

Black businesses prospered during the Jim Crow era for a couple of reasons. There was no competition from white businesses, and Black patrons wanted to boost their community. In addition, going to a white store could be dangerous. As segregation increased, more Black businesses were created to serve the community and to decrease the need to travel across the tracks. As Donna R. Braden, curator of public life at The Henry Ford, writes:

> OUT OF THE DEMEANING ENVIRONMENT OF JIM CROW arose the opportunity for some African Americans to establish their own businesses. The more cut off that black communities became from white communities and the more that white businessmen refused to cater to black customers, the more possible it became for enterprising black entrepreneurs to create viable businesses of their own.
>
> Most of these businesses were local, small-scale, and family run. Many black entrepreneurs followed the tenets of Booker T. Washington, who had established the National Business League in 1900 to promote economic self-help.[11]

This was happening in many areas across the South, where Jim Crow ruled with a heavy hand.

With the majority of the Black residents of the former Richmond County now located in Scotland County, there were new opportunities but also risks and potential pitfalls. Many of the white residents moved into Richmond County, where they enjoyed housing opportunities and voting privileges. Though members of the Black community had a culture of support and togetherness, they were still targets of racial violence. Using census reports, white supremacist groups knew the exact locations where most of the Black community lived. The residents of Scotland County had been a thorn in the supremacists' side for thirty years for avoiding separation, but now the county was in the bull's-eye.

―――

Though the Malloys and other families were making progress in securing their future in the early twentieth century, this was still a time of exodus from the South. The Great Migration began around 1910. With car factories and other industries booming in the North, many Black people headed in that direction during World War I. The word spread about opportunities in the Northern states through conversations and in advertisements in Black newspapers. Some people abandoned their properties in the South. Many others enlisted in the Army and went off to war. More than three hundred thousand Black people fought in World War I, over a hundred thousand more than in the Civil War, with more than two hundred thousand serving in Europe.[12] With no hesitation, Braxton put his education on hold and enlisted, becoming another Malloy to join the military and fight in a war.

In 1917, with Grace a toddler, Annie's daily life began to shift back to focus on church activities and other events. And then a few months later, she found herself pregnant with her fifth child, Lawrence, the eighth child in their continually growing family.

8. SOUTHERN TEA

"Seeds of Love," the title of a poem written by my mother, was inspired by my father's first biographical work by the same title. He toted the fifty-page document around under his arm as he walked the campus of Howard University on his way to his office at the bottom of the Blackburn Center. And he always had it with him when he visited friends in Kemp Mill or attended Alpha Phi Alpha gatherings and dances.

During these excursions, if someone were to engage in conversation with him while he had the autobiography with him, he or she would get an earful about family history. The conversation might start off with the usual pleasantries but eventually he would shift into his scripted responses such as: "Oh, my fault, my bag. Is that what they say now?" as he misinterpreted the popular saying. He would then present his mantra of sorts: "Don't you know me? I was the valedictorian at Laurinburg Institute. I sold cotton to all fifty states as a boy. My daddy and I owned the largest construction company and textile company in my town."

He would conclude by saying, "This is my book. It's self-published. Here, have a look." If the other party did indeed take the book, my father would eventually tell them, "Now give it back. I need that one. But if you want, I will get you a couple of copies. Yeah, let me get a couple copies to ya."

Folks were tickled and happy to receive a copy because they enjoyed his wit. My mother loved this about him. My father never seemed to have enough copies, or else he was trying to hold on to them. I once saw him bring four or five to my daughter's high school graduation. But after Uncle Donald, who was married to my mother's youngest sister Myrtle, asked for one, my father told everyone else who asked that he would have to get more for them another time. Uncle Donald held on to his copy, which decades later was the only one left in the family.

The spiral-bound booklet featured a photo of my father and mother on the cover, the same photo we submitted to the Presbyterian family directory for our church.

My father's book begins, "Autobiography of Lawrence E. Malloy, Sr. Born Colored." In our conversations on the leopard-print sofas in the second-floor living room, he would laugh and joke that he was the black sheep of his family. This statement would be followed by a vivid retelling of one of the many stories about his skin tone. He didn't joke about being the black sheep just because his skin was a few shades darker than his siblings'. My father's flamboyant style of dress, with big bow ties and flashy suits, was unlike the subdued attire usually worn by Malloy men. He was born colored, he claimed, but was listed as mulatto in the census of 1920 and as Black in later years.

Daddy would offer his advice freely. He often told us to live below our means. "Save the money you can spare to put in the bank with a good interest rate, and add to it as you can," he would advise. "But first, you have to make enough to be able to save enough."

When my father was putting together his autobiography, in the late 1960s, I asked, "Dad, can you put in your book how you made a lot of money and put some tips on how to increase it?" He replied, "Yeah, baby. You can read it, so you'll know how to handle things."

I couldn't wait to get my hands on his booklet to read the family secrets to wealth. When I was seven, I filled my green mouse-shaped papier-mâché bank with any money that came my way from chores, allowance, and lunch money, accumulating five hundred dollars by the time I was twelve. After I read his book, I saw that he hadn't included the secrets to financial success, but instead discussed the strategic positioning of the Malloys in different fields and their deep connection to education, from Laurinburg to Washington, DC. His book spiked my interest in Laurinburg, and I was eager to encounter the setting of his stories.

My first trip to Laurinburg was too quiet for comfort. The town felt like traveling back in time. Respect for elders and their families' contributions had been preserved. It was also a place that allowed you to take in the beauty of God's green horizons. It seemed that everyone was rich, no matter their income or the size of their home. In Laurinburg, it was the foundation and roots of the community that mattered.

Odessa Shaw Smith, who we all called Aunt Dess, Daddy's sister from my grandfather's last marriage, lived in a small house of no more than eight hundred square feet on Dixon Street. The house, built by my grandfather's hands, stood tall for decades until 2020, when it burned down. We are not sure what caused the fire. It took literal fires, bombs, or torrential weather to take down prosperous towns built by Black hands between Reconstruction and the 1950s.

I got to see the inner workings of the Laurinburg community as a child. I saw that the community was a big family roaming throughout each other's homes in what my mom called the "round robin." Everyone seemed to agree that "my house is your house." When we went to Aunt Dess's house, I would see the same neighbor I had seen the day before at another relative's house, as well as others who looked very comfortable in each location.

My relatives all knew the troubled history behind the land they were living on. Black communities were numerous in the south part of the state. Halifax County, Scotland County, and Robeson County, on the border of South Carolina, had the largest populations of free Black people dating back to slavery. Though the communities in the South were supportive of each other, the Great Migration started a pattern that continued after the initial rush of four hundred thousand leaving the South.

In 1918, the world was reeling from the Spanish flu, which had taken lives in the United States since March. It was the first pandemic since the bubonic plague and its aftermath.[1] In September, it reached North Carolina. Many in the state had been infected with viruses before, but nothing like this.

Unlike pneumonia and tuberculosis, this virus targeted young adults, putting them at the highest risk of death. Even with William and other doctors in the family, no one was safe in this first H1N1 pandemic. In addition, World War I was still raging, with 104 Black doctors serving alongside 40,000 Black troops.

My uncle Braxton was part of Company H of the 807th Pioneer Infantry Regiment. He was inducted on July 18, 1918, and was shipped to Paris on September 4, 1918.[2] While in Paris, his infantry was part of the Meuse–Argonne Offensive, the final offense of the war, which drove the Germans out of France.

The war ended with an armistice on November 11, 1918. With hospitals crowded and the death toll rising from the pandemic, it was a difficult time to have a child. The end of the war was a relief. Soldiers returned home, and rationing rules, like the ones regulating the purchase of sugar, were lifted. The cost of the First World War was immense. Worldwide, 9 million soldiers had died, and 21 million were wounded. Among the dead were 116,516 US soldiers—2,188 of them from North Carolina.

On December 18, 1918, just weeks after the armistice, Annie delivered Lawrence Edward Malloy, my father and the eighth child in the family. When a baby was born, the entire family showed up to the house to welcome the newborn. Braxton was still overseas and was not discharged until July 16, 1919.[3] Leland, Zelda, Emmett, Dot, Mae, and two-year-old Grace were in the room to meet their new sibling. They kissed Annie and the baby. Lawrence was a few shades darker than his brothers. This was not something they instantly noticed or were concerned with as a family, but William knew his son would automatically have an experience different from his brothers.

As soon as Lawrence could walk and talk, Annie and his siblings became his teachers. By age five, he was learning his multiplication tables and could recite them by memory. He would practice as if learning lines from Shakespeare, performing the tables aloud for the family. Grace, only two years older, was his playmate and partner in crime. Dot, who was a few years older and had a bossy personality, leaned into her older sibling status and made sure they stayed on task.

Emmett was now an undergrad studying biology at Johnson C. Smith University, an HBCU located about a hundred miles from Laurinburg, a two-and-a-half-hour drive on back roads. The university was established as Freedmen's College of North Carolina, and then the name was changed to Biddle Memorial Institute. The current name was adopted in 1923.

During Emmett's attendance, the North Carolina Board of Education sanctioned the school as a four-year college. With the war over, Braxton returned to school at Meharry, finishing his medical degree in 1923. He set his sights on the Midwest and found work as a general practice physician in Massillon, Ohio.

In 1926, Emmett received his bachelor of science degree from Johnson C. Smith University, the same school where William's brother Darius would send his son Rembert Malloy five years later. The 1926 yearbook includes this about Emmett: "LAURINBURG, N.C. 'Foots,' 'Sticks,' and 'Mack' Malloy are all the one and same. He hails from the Scotch section of the Old North State, which is exemplified by his penuriousness. . . . 'Mack' is a conscientious student and plans to take dentistry. He will become one of the hoity toity opulent class as soon as he discovers an alloy of one per cent gold and ninety nine percent Scotland County Clay." Emmett continued his studies, moving into dentistry.

With the buzzing of the Harlem Renaissance heard all the way to the South, Leland took the carpentry skills he learned from his father and his medical degree to New York City, where he quickly started working as a carpenter in Harlem.

With Braxton, Leland, and Emmett out of the house, Lawrence was the only boy. His sisters Fairley Mae and Grace were attending Laurinburg Institute. Before becoming a teacher at Laurinburg, Dot attended Barber-Scotia College in Concord, North Carolina, an HBCU commissioned by the Presbyterian Church to train Black women in education and social work. Prestigious graduates included educator and civil rights leader Mary

McLeod Bethune; Katie Cannon, the first African American woman ordained in the Presbyterian Church; women's rights advocate and educator Ellen E. Armstrong; and later, Pulitzer Prize–nominated poet Vivian Ayers Allen. In the 1930s, Barber-Scotia Junior College was a stepping stone to Johnson C. Smith College. If you finished at Barber-Scotia, you were eligible for Johnson C. Smith.[4]

Though Lawrence was younger, his father always told him, "Take care of your sisters." My father walked Grace to school and looked out for her during the school day. He loved his studies and sports, especially baseball, but his father was very keen on sports only as a leisure activity or hobby. Lawrence took notice of the Negro League's teams, such as the Charlotte Black Hornets, and played many days to sharpen his skills on the field.

Since he was the youngest and his grandmother Eliza was getting up in age, Lawrence didn't spend as much time with her as his older siblings did. One day, when he was seven or eight, he put on his best knickers and jumped into the family's car, the only one in the community. He watched through the window as the striped lawns and homes, some of which had been made by his daddy's hands, popped into view. Fifteen to twenty minutes after getting on the dirt roads, they turned down a long driveway to a house Lawrence had not seen before. He knew he was going to visit his grandmother in Laurel Hill. He looked forward to reciting his times tables and, if time allowed, a few scriptures.

William exited the car first and went to the front door of the palatial front porch. Lawrence opened his door and jumped down with a swift step and followed his father. Another set of visitors were at the home: the white relatives, the descendants of Daniel Murdock's half brothers and sisters. Laying eyes on Lawrence, they proceeded to call out, "Get that Black boy off my lawn."

My father's darker skin tone put him at risk, even from his own kin.

Within seconds, Lawrence took off running, even faster than he did on the baseball field. Their hate-filled vitriol sent fear throughout his body. He ran as if his life depended on it. When he glanced back and saw his relatives bearing a pitchfork just a sprint away, he ran even faster. As my father ran through the meticulous yard, landscaped with beds of geraniums and petunias, he saw a wooden shack and ran inside. Once inside, he hid in a haystack until he fell asleep from exhaustion.

For a while, they couldn't find him. But after the opening door woke him, he saw his relatives hovering over him with a pitchfork in hand. William opened the door and stopped them in the act. Since he was a boy, he was never privy to the conversations among the adults after that incident.

Though his visit to Eliza eventually ended with a nice lunch, the chase was imprinted in his thoughts as a traumatic stressor, ready to be ignited at any moment in his life. The Fermata Psychotherapy center in Chicago states: "Complex trauma can . . . alter our sense of time by making us feel that past, present, and future are disconnected from one another."[5] As an adult, my father always stopped telling this story after the part where he was discovered in the haystack. He would skip the visit to his grandmother and instead exclaim about her beauty.

My father wasn't sent to therapy. In that era, the church and the family played that role for those who suffered traumatic experiences. The common wisdom was that you prayed and kept moving.

Lawrence's uncle Arthur also lived in Laurel Hill at that time. It would have been an insult for Arthur not to stop by when his brother William brought my father for visits to Laurel Hill. The brothers were spread throughout the state, with Darius moving to Winston-Salem. This did not deter William from staying in Laurinburg.

After that first trip to Laurel Hill, my father had more appreciation for Laurinburg and the comfort it offered him, living in a community that knew who he was. Though Laurinburg still had its racial challenges, it seemed better than Laurel Hill. In Laurel Hill, stories in the white community celebrated the death and torture of Black people. One such legend praised a community member who, during a fight, mutilated a Black man who was said to be a wanted criminal from South Carolina.

William and his family lived in the Stewartsville township of Scotland County. Consisting of eighty-one of the three hundred and twenty square miles of Scotland County, Stewartsville was a mix of farmland and homes. Scotland County was in the southeast region of the Piedmont Plateau area of North Carolina, which bordered South Carolina. Richmond County, which used to encompass this area, was in the eastern region of the plateau.

In the mid-twentieth century, cotton still reigned supreme in the county, but agriculture was increasing at a higher rate than in most other states across the country. The average cotton yield was $76.12 per acre (equivalent to $1,367.43 in 2024). Livestock, watermelons, cantaloupes, peaches, acid phosphate, cotton seed, flour, and coal were starting to compete with the output of cotton.

In 1924, Laurinburg High School was built. There was increased pride in town. Other than the insurrection, Laurinburg was a quiet town. A murder or any type of non-natural death was a scandalous situation. While the carnival coming to town would cause extreme excitement, the mummified body of carnival worker Cancetto

Farmica, whose skull was crushed with a metal tent stake wielded by a coworker, was a bigger attraction and the first time the town made national news. In 1911, at age twenty-three, he died as a result of the injury after a long ride to James Sanatorium in Laurinburg. His family asked that McDougald's Funeral Home keep the body until they could afford to bring their son home to Sicily.

The Laurinburg Exchange reported, "Farmica's embalmed body mummified—or dried out—and was hung by a rope across his chest and under his arms in the third-story embalming room at M.A. McDougald." The locals gave him the nickname "Spaghetti" due to his Italian origins. Eventually the body was put into a box.[6] Sixty years later, a New York congressman who found out about the story thought the treatment of Farmica was discriminatory and paid for his burial.

Day by day, the town was flourishing. In 1924, in a newspaper article titled "Things You Want to Know About Scotland County," Herbert K. Fox, the executive secretary of the Scotland County Chamber of Commerce, celebrated its riches, including the pleasant weather and the state-of-the-art water-filtration system:

> THE HOMES TO BE FOUND IN THE COUNTY rank among the best of the entire country. In the towns are to be found sufficient water, electric lights, telephones as is the case all over the county and in Laurinburg, concrete sidewalks, adequate sewerage and paved streets. . . . There are 42 schools with 129 teachers, school population of 5,686 or 86 percent of the entire population. . . . The value of the school property is $879,400 . . . and a private negro industrial school valued at approximately $100,000. In recreation Laurinburg has an enclosed ball park, golf links and other means of enjoyment. Bathing in this section is a great sport. The women have their

home demonstration work and other recreational activities. There are churches of all leading denominations. . . . Most productive county in relation to rise of farm area of any county in the United States. Population (estimated 1923) 3000. Eight manufacturing plants, including 4 large cotton mills.[7]

'The people of the town cooperated with one another to push Laurinburg's productivity ahead of that of other areas. Many banks and the Chamber of Commerce had their headquarters in Laurinburg, the county seat.

Laurinburg Institute, which was within walking distance, was a second home for my father. The entire community welcomed the school. Emmanuel and Tinny McDuffie, along with other members of the community, cleared the original land by hand. The $100,000 valuation of the school in 1924 would be equivalent to more than $1.8 million today. In 1924, the school received accreditation from the state. It was the only high school for Black students in the city.

Lawrence loved school and a range of topics from carpentry, math, and English to music. He felt fulfilled shifting from homeschooling to joining students his age who were also furthering their knowledge and looked like him.

William was becoming more involved in the church. Bowers Chapel was his home away from home. Wealthy Black community members such as Walter P. Evans were also members. William started teaching Sunday school and ran for office at the Yadkin Eastern District Sunday School Conventions. The Yadkin Presbytery consisted of Black church elders and ministers who represented the congregations in the area. At the Eastern District

Sunday School Conventions, various Sunday schools could represent their churches among their peers. It was also a chance for teachers to share their lessons and updates. Black Presbyterians traveled from all over to attend these conventions, which included formal programs with performances and presentations. William was elected superintendent at the 1925 convention, which took place forty-one miles away in Carthage, North Carolina.

The Africo-American Presbyterian, a weekly newspaper founded in 1879 and based in Wilmington, North Carolina, kept track of the happenings within the Black Presbyterian community and reported national news that affected the Black community.[8] Bowers Chapel was often mentioned, as was the Malloy family.

William continued to expand his roles, running for other positions—and winning. Articles in 1925 and 1926 about the Eastern District Sunday School Convention read: "The popular program on Friday evening was a splendid success conducted by Vice President WM Malloy,"[9] and "At the popular meeting at 8pm, our program was climaxed with the address of Superintendent WM Malloy. The address was very helpful as the speaker pointed out very plainly what we must do to improve the convention."[10]

The members of the presbytery would visit Laurinburg and have a gathering after church at William's house on Dixon Street. In the one photo that exists, the men of the presbytery are all dressed in the finest suits, and with the exception of one of the fifty, none wore a smile. William's connection to the church, Sunday school, and presbytery gave him a new lease on life.

When Lawrence was nine, his mother, Annie, started feeling ill. William was alarmed by the unhealthy yellow hue of her skin. By 1927, William's brother Darius was building a reputation as a prominent doctor in Winston-Salem and had a nice life with his wife, Laney. Braxton was practicing in Massillon, Ohio, so they were too distanced to help Annie, and this was beyond what William was able to address as she progressed.

At times, Annie seemed to improve, but then she regressed. Dot and Zelda helped where they could. When Annie's symptoms got worse, William took his wife an hour away to Highsmith Hospital in Fayetteville, North Carolina. There were no Black doctors there, but they did have state-of-the-art facilities and a hundred beds. It was said that private hospitals were less likely to follow the racist behavior of public hospitals, or they were at least more subtle. Highsmith was the first private hospital and nursing school in North Carolina and had just moved to a new location two years prior.

At Highsmith, Annie was diagnosed with cholecystitis of the gallbladder, a silent illness until it becomes dire. She immediately underwent surgery on her gallbladder, which had burst. She was kept at the hospital. With Grace and Lawrence still at home, Dot, who lived nearby and was their teacher at Laurinburg Institute, stepped into mother mode.

The weeks and months rushed by, but Annie did not improve. Unfortunately, the surgery did not correct the condition, and after a series of complications, including liver shock, Annie passed away on August 6, 1928. One census said she was born in 1883; however, her death certificate stated she died at age forty-nine in 1928. We have not been able to locate a birth certificate. *The New York Age* published an article that highlighted her life:

> **MRS. ANNIE MALLOY WIFE OF W.M. MALLOY,** a well-known citizen of Laurinburg and Scotland County passed to the great beyond Monday, August 6, at the Highsmith Hospital in Fayetteville, N.C., where she underwent a serious operation several weeks ago. Mrs. Malloy had been failing in health for more than a year and so the end was not expected, yet it was a

shock to everybody to learn of her death. She was a splendid member of society and an untiring church worker. Most of her time was spent rearing a family of useful and law-abiding children, three stepchildren and five children of her own.

    The eldest Dr. W B Malloy is a practicing physician in Massalia, [sic] Ohio; Lelan [sic] Malloy, carpenter of New York City; Mrs. Zelda Malloy Johnson of Laurinburg, Dorothy D. Malloy teacher at Laurinburg Institute, Emmett Malloy student at J. C. Smith University, Charlotte, N.C.; Fairley Mae Malloy recent graduate of Laurinburg Institute; Grace Malloy and Lawrence, children yet in their teens. Funeral services were held at the Bowers Chapel Presbyterian Church Wednesday at three o clock. . . . The body was laid to rest in the cemetery of this city. The McDougald Undertaking establishment of Laurinburg had charge of the burial. She left six sisters, eight children, a husband, and a host of friends to mourn their loss.[11]

After Annie's death, joy in the home diminished. A few months shy of turning ten, Lawrence mourned with the family. The Malloy men were not afraid of tears but did not dwell on their grief. Lawrence went back to school, and everyone went to work shortly after, fearful of losing time and progress.

A few years later, Laurinburg Institute informed the Malloy family that a new student, who was on scholarship, needed a place to stay near the campus. The rooms were full at the time. The Malloys opened their doors to a young man named John Birks. This was the first time there was another boy Lawrence's age in the house. The fourteen-year-olds went to school together, and both played trumpet in music class. This new friendship restored some of the joy in the household, as they were also pranksters. Lawrence's first best friend would later be known as Dizzy Gillespie.

9. COMING OF AGE

Whenever Dizzy Gillespie came to Washington, DC, it was a big event for my family. In the fifties, my father would invite all his nearby friends and family to the row house on Ames Street in the River Terrace corridor where he lived with my mother and brother Leon. These were exciting times during which the community gathered, as they did in Laurinburg, for fellowship with one another. Legal school segregation across the country had ended in 1954, ten years prior to the passage of the Civil Rights Act. Our community and schools were majority Black, and many people worked for the federal government.

Mailed paper invitations promised guests a delicious Southern-style meal, perhaps featuring my mother's tasty fried pork chops and Dad's amazing T-bone steaks or burnt hot dogs with toasted buns. While the rest of the food was cooking, my father mixed A.1. Sauce with mustard, ketchup, and barbecue sauce, creating his own special sauce that sizzled in a pot on the grill for all to use at their leisure on the steaks, hot dogs, and more in the cemented backyard. Some of the guests would enjoy a few highball cocktails.

Then after socializing, my mother and father would walk arm in arm with Aunt Grace and Aunt Dot and Uncle Oliver to avoid stumbles. Fancy Aunt Mae came from New York City with her husband, Dave, who dressed in a preppy style as if he had just walked off an Ivy League campus. They, too, proceeded arm in arm. Family friends—the Walls, the Moores, Cousin Tom Milton and his wife, the Gibsons, and the McLaurins, who also lived in the district—strolled slowly into the living room and perched on the hand-crafted couches around the upright piano.

By the late fifties, Dizzy Gillespie was a household name. Known as the Ambassador of Jazz, he was a pioneer of the syncopated, exciting genre known as bebop. He had recorded several albums, toured the world, and had hits such as "Salt Peanuts." He was a unique trumpet player who not only pioneered new forms of jazz but also became known for his personal playing style, which involved puffed cheeks and a trumpet with a bell that turned upward (it had been damaged in an accident). The bent horn produced a sound he loved, and it became his trademark.

With his humble smile and laid-back charm, Dizzy would make his way to my parents' living room piano. All eyes zoomed in for this private privilege. A multi-instrumentalist, he played a jazz tune on the piano while my mother sang, dressed in one of her many dresses that looked as if they came from the set of *I Love Lucy*. Her vibrant voice lit up the room. She smiled through her notes, infectiously spreading joy. She was in her element with one of the greatest. The next day or night, we would attend Dizzy's show. His visits were inevitably connected to a live show, which was always a treat for me to attend.

I started playing the drums when I was ten. I was already learning the guitar and was ready to move on to the next instrument so I could become my own band, adding music to my poetry without leaning on any other musicians. Heading to Dizzy's show on another one of his visits, I didn't really understand the importance of the occasion. I knew we were all dressed up alike in sparkling Nehru suits, which were in style, and looked like the 5th Dimension or the Partridge Family. I thought we might be going onstage.

Now living in Maryland, we drove a few miles down the street to a club that was also in Silver Spring, only ten minutes from the city. My ears opened as I listened to the cacophony of sounds and melodies improvised and mixed with Latin genres. As a young artist, I had my perspective broadened. This was a style of jazz focused on improvisation and solos.

In between sets, I walked up to world-renowned jazz drummer Max Roach, who not only played for many greats but was also featured in one of my favorite films *Carmen Jones*, which starred Dorothy Dandridge and Harry Belafonte. I walked onto the stage as if I belonged because I was accustomed to doing so at my mother's performances. I told him I played, and he let me sit at the drums for a bit. Nerves prevented me from doing much, but it was enough for Mr. Roach to give me his sticks, which I would later pass on to my daughter while teaching her how to play.

When I finished, a woman in the audience told me, "You don't know how lucky you are." No doubt this was true. I was simply accustomed to these occasions, as was my family. My cousins and aunts and uncles all knew Dizzy as my father's best friend since childhood.

In my cousin Tootles's collection of photos, there was one of Dizzy hanging out in our DC backyard. He knew our tight-knit family from the Laurinburg days, and they all considered him family. While digging through genealogical research I discovered that we were in fact cousins. My father may not have known this, but either way, Dizzy was family by way of love.

When my daughter was four, Dizzy happened to be in town to go to a private screening of the film *'Round Midnight*, directed by Bertrand Tavernier, with music by Herbie Hancock. The premiere, which we would also be attending with my parents, was held at the Kennedy Center in a hidden backstage area. Now my daughter would be meeting him for the second time. Though she wasn't a jazz enthusiast at age four, she was excited to meet Dizzy because of his appearance on one of her favorite television programs, *The Cosby Show*.

Prior to the screening, we visited Dizzy's Georgetown hotel, tagging along with my dad. I wanted to play Dizzy some of the music I was working on. Right away, my daughter saw his big cheeks and asked if he personally knew Rudy from *The Cosby Show*. He was startled that she asked about other celebrities first. He said, "Well, that was rude. You say hello first!"

I knew this was my fault. I had gotten her excited about his television experiences with her favorite child star, so she was too geared up to even greet Dizzy. After she did so, the two of them talked about television, *Sesame Street*, and the miniature refrigerator in Dizzy's hotel room, which my daughter had never seen before.

I played him some of my songs, and Dizzy complimented them, then asked where the jazz was, because to him bebop was really jazz. At that point in my career, I played jazz by rote, listening to Dizzy and his peers such as Ella Fitzgerald, Boz Scaggs, Lionel Hampton, and Nancy Wilson on my record player, which had a penny taped to the needle to keep the sounds smooth with the needle pressed to the record. With Dizzy's comment, I thought to myself, I need to revisit my concept of jazz. Later, when I went back to Howard University, I studied with recording artist Grady

Tate, Ella Fitzgerald's band director, who was taught by the same music teacher as my father and Dizzy.

After my daughter told Dizzy she had just had a birthday, he replied that his was coming up in two weeks: They had a Libra connection. He was jovial and fun, and she smiled the entire time. I was happy she was getting the same experience with Dizzy Gillespie that I'd had growing up.

Time passed quickly as we watched the film. Although Dizzy wasn't in the movie but was honored in it, my mother asked everyone to give another round of applause for John Birks, the name Dizzy required his friends to call him. On the way to the after-party in another section of the Kennedy Center, Dizzy was presented with a bouquet of balloons. A balloon in the shape of a cake caught my daughter's eye. Since it had just been her birthday, Dizzy gave her all of his balloons.

Her face lit up until his agent asked her why she had them. Dizzy quickly let him know they were hers. His agent said, "It's okay, this is the next big star right here," prompting another smile from my young daughter.

During the after-party, my father insisted on filming everyone. He wanted them to say their name and what they did so he could share the film with his beloved Howard University employees. With Dizzy on camera, my father said in his fully projected Southern twang, "This is Dr. Dizzy Gillespie. We went to Laurinburg Normal High School together. I would've never imagined Dr. Dizzy Gillespie would be speaking at . . ."

Dizzy cut him off to laughter: "Don't tell that story! Oh boy!" Later when my father asked him to visit Howard University, Dizzy said he was too busy. My mother followed up in her congenial way, knowing my father could be insistent. "Only if you want to, Dizzy," she said.

Then my father said in the same tone, "No, I want you to. The agent can schedule it."

Dizzy nodded and continued to tell a joke. He was among a small group of close friends of my father's who dated back to his days at Laurinburg Institute, including Mr. Mac, his brother Dan, the Gibson family, and a lady named McRae, all of whom came from prominent families in Laurinburg.

———

Many years after both Dizzy and my father had died, my daughter and I were driving in Maryland when she had to use the restroom. We pulled over at a library we had never seen. We walked around and saw that they had a video-restoration station. Of all the videos my father had recorded, we ended up with just one in our possession. Later, we returned to the restoration station and nervously popped the VHS tape into the machine, knowing it might be the only video record of my father.

As the video played, we saw decades of my father's life and times in one hour. He loved to clip and splice his videos. The family room was his own recording studio, and the videotapes sat on the broken television console that he had promised to fix for years. The scenes flashed past: my parents dancing at a wedding; my mother's graduation; my mother receiving her master's degree and hugging Sammy Davis Jr., who posed with her choir; a ceremony at Howard University honoring my father; my daughter's dance recital; and the day Dizzy visited for the film screening. In the video, you can see the brotherhood of Dizzy and my father: their smiles, their jokes, their sarcasm, and their love.

The brotherly bond between my father and Dizzy Gillespie stemmed from the connection built at the Black boarding school that allowed Black boys to be teenagers in a world that often forced them to grow up too soon. Dizzy's father passed away one year before my grandmother Annie. Both boys had endured the loss of a parent before they met; and since Dizzy was one of nine, he too knew about life in a large family.

The economy was also in a new place at this time. The Great Depression affected everyone as well as the banks. Per the book *Terry Sanford: Politics, Progress, and Outrageous Ambitions*: "After O. Max Gardner took office as North Carolina's governor in January 1929, he immediately began to marshal the state's resources."[1] The book later states "Laurinburg lost two institutions, The First National Bank and Scotland Savings."[2] But because of the circular connection feeding back into Black businesses, many Laurinburg entrepreneurs protected themselves from some of the financial hits others suffered during the Depression.

Education remained central for the Malloys. In 1929, *The New York Age* stated, "Friends of Will Malloy, leading carpenter of this town, will rejoice heartily with him over the graduation of his son, Emmett from Johnson C. Smith University, June 6. Mr. Malloy and the entire family motored to Charlotte and were present for the exercises. Emmett is spending a few days at home and will leave for New York City in the near future."[3] The youngest Malloy, Lawrence, was also well into his education.

In 1932, when my dad and Dizzy were students, Laurinburg Institute was moving into a new era, with new funding and renovations: "By 1932, Laurinburg Institute had been transformed from a single building to a thriving school complex. On the former swampland stood 14 buildings that, together with the school's livestock, were estimated to represent up to $250,000 in assets. Twenty-seven teachers instructed 684 enrolled students; graduates operated the Hallowell-Wellington Kindergarten for black children."[4]

When he arrived, Dizzy was stepping into an education he had never experienced as a Black boy in the South. As he observed in his memoir, *To Be, or Not . . . to Bop*, "During the orientation tour of the campus, Laurinburg seemed like a complete little town. They had classrooms . . . dorms for boys and girls, a large football field and outside basketball courts, a hospital, and an administration building."[5]

The teachers at the school were experts in their subjects. The band teacher, Philmore "Shorty" Hall, referred to as Maestro Hall by Dizzy, had been a recording artist with Black Birds of Paradise from Montgomery, Alabama, a popular early jazz band active from 1925 to 1931. The Great Depression halted the fame of his group, providing fewer opportunities, and he settled in North Carolina to teach in Laurinburg. There he developed a reputation for training Dizzy before moving to other schools and training other jazz legends such as Grady Tate.

Aunt Dot taught English at Laurinburg and ran her classroom as she ran her household: strictly but with a smile. Having no children of her own, teaching was her connection to motherhood, as was helping Grace and Lawrence when Annie passed away.

At school, Lawrence and Dizzy both had to learn a trade. Classes like agriculture were easy for them since both grew up farming. The two of them also got jobs. Lawrence worked with W. M. Malloy and Son, his father's construction company, while

Dizzy worked on a farm. Since Laurinburg was such a large farm community, it was easy for a teenage boy to find work on the land. For years, Dizzy picked cotton.

In the book *Groovin' High: The Life of Dizzy Gillespie*, author Alyn Shipton writes, "The farm was the easiest and most obvious source of sufficient extra income to pay for clothes and shoes, and [Dizzy] spent the entire summer . . . between semesters working there."[6] After three years at Laurinburg, Dizzy left to pursue his music full-time.

When not in class, playing sports, or working, the two teenage boys were cracking jokes and having fun at my father's house, which was known in the community as the White House on the Hill, a fun place to be sure. Backyard tennis matches featured pop-up appearances from famous Black players like Nathaniel Jackson.

The Jackson family, which still owns property in Laurinburg, was making waves in the community in the thirties. Nathaniel and his brother Franklyn both grew up in Laurinburg, and by 1932 they were American Tennis Association national doubles champions. Though he eventually moved to Wilmington, Nathaniel kept a family home in Laurinburg and made the town proud. His winning streak kept going for the next seven years. When he returned home from Wilmington, it was a grand occasion. In later years he would practice with the likes of Althea Gibson.

Another Jackson, possibly from the same family, Dr. N. E. Jackson, ran Bigelow Hospital, which operated on the grounds of Laurinburg Institute beginning in 1926. Though the hospital was no anomaly, it was "one of the least known African American hospitals in North Carolina," according to retired nurse and author Phoebe Ann Pollitt. "Available records indicate it operated from the mid-1920s until the 1950s. Even the dates of its founding and demise are not well documented. Brief mentions in a few newspapers, a designation on a map and a background image in a 1920s photograph of Laurinburg Institute students are all that is left to tell the story of Bigelow Hospital."[7]

In 1932, William began courting Miss Hattie Shaw. Her grandson Wilbur Malloy told me about her:

> SHE HAD A LOT OF ACRES. By the standards of the community, she was well off. She was the only Black female landowner or farmer with significant acreage. She never worked outside of the home and had a full-time housekeeper. She raised eight girls and a boy during the Depression. Her first husband died in 1927 and left her with nine children. Seven of them went to college and graduated, the other two at least had some college.[8]

In 1934, William and Hattie Shaw were married. The groom was about sixty-nine and the bride was forty-seven. It's likely that the wedding took place at Bowers Chapel. This was William's third marriage. Hattie was his first wife to have been previously married, and she had children, making William now the father of seventeen.

Aunt Dot, now married to Oliver Robinson, a member of the Freemason Society, moved to Washington, DC, in the early 1930s to start a new life. By 1932, she was settled in the city working as a domestic, the same role she witnessed her mother doing in Laurinburg. The move to DC did not stop her from visiting Laurinburg every chance she got. The July 30, 1932, edition of *The New York Age* reported: "Mrs. Dorothy Malloy Robinson, daughter of Will Malloy of the town who is now living in Washington, D.C., is spending time at her former home here. Mrs. Robinson is a graduate of the Institute and was a member of the faculty for several years."[9]

Lawrence's sister Fairley Mae also made her way to a new state. The October 8, 1932, edition of *The New York Age* shared her visit home: "Miss Fairley Mae Malloy, daughter of W. Malloy of Laurinburg, a member of the class of '28 of Laurinburg Institute and a February graduate of the school of Nursing of Dixie Hospital Hampton Institute VA., is at home for a short while. Since her graduation at Hampton, she has been on the staff of Nurses at the Dixie Hospital."[10]

Though everyday life was going well in the Malloy house, not too far away in Laurel Hill, William's brother Arthur passed away. "Arthur Malloy, brother of Will Malloy of this town, died at his home in Laurel Hill, N.C. last week," *The New York Age* reported. "He was well known by the people of Scotland County generally and was from one of the oldest and distinguished families of this section. Dr. H. D. Malloy and family of Winston-Salem, N. C. were in town last week on the occasion of the death of the doctor's brother Arthur who passed away last week and was laid to rest in the Morgan Cemetery."[11]

The political climate was changing as well. Though most in the Black community were supporters of Democrat Al Smith because of his religious background and his progressive stance on suffrage and prohibition, they could not outnumber the supporters of Republican Herbert Hoover, who took the election in

North Carolina and in the United States in 1928. It had been the first time a Republican had won in North Carolina since 1872.

By the next presidential election in 1932, 75 percent of Black voters had moved to the Democratic Party because of Franklin D. Roosevelt's campaign and promise of many programs to provide relief. The community was getting very little from the Republican Party and was ready for change. In North Carolina's race for governor, Democratic nominee John C. B. Ehringhaus defeated Republican Clifford C. Frazier with 70 percent of the vote.

In 1934, 500 workers at textile mills in East Laurinburg went on strike due to poor working conditions. The strike became violent with many suffering from gunshot wounds. Due to the large number of protesters the strike was in the news across the state and gaining more media attention. The strike was not resolved until there was mediation with both sides.[12]

Meanwhile, in Winston-Salem, Dr. Henry Darius Malloy was operating the only Black practice dedicated to surgery. Whenever Darius visited Laurinburg, William was eager to brag about his little brother. In October 1934, *The Africo-American Presbyterian* reported on Darius's visit with William to the homecoming service of Chapel Hill Church:

> DIRECTLY AFTER THE SERMON MR. WILLIAM MALLOY of Bowers' Chapel church, Laurinburg, introduced his brother, Doctor Malloy, of Winston Salem, both being former members of Chapel Hill church. . . . Mr. Malloy gave Dr. Malloy the opportunity to speak in his own way. Dr. Malloy gave a brief history of old Chapel Hill church. He said he had come back home to the scenes of his childhood. It was there that he went to school and church from his youth up to young manhood. Therefore, it is only natural

that the church and grounds should have peculiar charm for him. . . . We wish to extend a hearty welcome to Mrs. Malloy to visit us at any time for we believe that Dr. Malloy's success is due largely to her loyalty and love.[13]

Lawerence would be the last Malloy to graduate from Laurinburg Institute, and all members of the family returned to celebrate him. *The Africo-American Presbyterian* captured the moment in its June 13, 1935, edition: "Mr. and Mrs. Oliver Robinson, of Washington, accompanied by their sister Grace Malloy, were here to witness the commencement exercise at Laurinburg Institute, and to see their brother Lorence [Lawrence] graduate. Mr. and Mrs. Robinson visited many of their friends and relatives while here. Miss Malloy spent most of her time with her father, Mr. W.M. Malloy."[14]

A few years later, another member of Bowers Chapel Church, Walter P. Evans, the well-known entrepreneur, passed away on February 27, 1937. "Mr. Evans was an outstanding-colored man in the state of North Carolina," reported his obituary in *The Africo-American Presbyterian*:

> **HE HAD A DETERMINATION TO SUCCEED** in business. He was a merchant for 40 years and was also in the wood and coal business. At one time he had control of a 14-horse farm and at the time of his death he was in possession of a 10-horse farm. He built a three-story brick store on Main Street in

> Laurinburg. At that time this was one of the prettiest buildings on Main Street, it was called W P Evans white storefront. During the depression, Mr. Evans tried to take care of the farmers, as he had done for many years before. But unfortunately, he had to give what he had to pay for what they had used. Closing the white store front, he conducted a grocery store in the same building. For two years prior to his illness, he operated a 10-horse farm which he purchased since the Depression. Mr. Evans was born in Wilmington, NC in the year 1863. . . . He was married twice. His first wife was Mrs. Josephine Meares Evans of Wilmington. She was burned to death in the store some years ago during Christmas time. Later he married again. . . . Mr. Evans served his community, town, church, and friends. He was well thought of by both white and colored.[15]

With leaders such as Evans passing away, it was now time for Lawrence to follow in the steps of his brothers and attend college to become a doctor. The Great Migration, the Depression, and integration had caused shifts for some businesses in the Black community. Some closed and others left for bigger opportunities. When it was Lawrence's turn to attend college, William, who had had many children to support, was left with less than expected for his baby boy. Hattie's children were mostly adults at this point, and she sent them to college with her own money.

Lawrence took a job at a local beer garden. He loved serving customers and making sure the space was safe for them. A young man, but full grown at this point, he knew how to shoot a pistol and rarely operated in fear. He walked the garden during its operating hours, keeping a watchful eye for anyone stepping out of line, drinking too much, or coming onto the premises with ill intent. Thanks to the skill set Lawrence had acquired working on the farm and with his father, he quickly moved up to management. This was the first time a young Black man in Laurinburg had a leadership role in an integrated business.

Much like the parties at the Malloy family home, the beer garden became a hub for gatherings. Musicians from the school band played while the beer and appetizers flowed through the space, which had a scenic background of bald cypress trees. And in the midst of it all, Lawrence was the king of hospitality. With a smile from cheek to cheek, he would call out to arriving customers: "Hello! Welcome! Please enjoy yourself!" As a manager, he made sure that everyone on the workforce was meeting their marks. He knew the power of word of mouth in his community: If this integrated business succeeded amid Jim Crow, it could change the culture of the land.

The white supremacist groups that had mounted the local insurrection during Reconstruction were still lurking in the swampland, popping up from time to time to fight people of color and their allies, and burn or damage Black-owned properties or businesses that supported the Black community. Decades after they ripped and roared through Scotland County, a group of men found out about the oasis of a beer garden under Lawrence's management. Members of a local supremacist group showed up at the entrance, yelling and screaming. Instead of a smile, they were greeted by my father's rifle. Though the men fled, Lawrence's days at the beer garden were numbered. He was ready for his next adventure.

My father went back to focusing solely on working construction with his father's company to earn extra money for college. He also started teaching building and contracting at Laurinburg Institute.

Since Grace had moved to Washington, DC, to be with her sister Dot and to work in the government, Lawrence and Zelda were the only children, by blood, of William's who were at home at 215 Dixon Street. This would not be for long, though, after World War II broke out. Lawrence enlisted at age twenty-one, with William indicated on his military card as both his employer and the person who would know his address.

Assigned to building bombs and engineering, Lawrence found new friends among his Army comrades. He learned French while in Paris. This was his first time outside the United States. According to his autobiography, Lawrence served for five years, first as a staff sergeant for the School of Intelligence (serving three years with the infantry) and then overseas with the Ordinance Ammunition Company as a supply sergeant.

My father spoke about spending time in Paris during the war, the only time he traveled to Europe. All the soldiers had to pass through the building where he typically worked to get to the front lines. One day, a warning siren signaled an incoming bomb. Lawrence was in the field with a close friend and ran over to join him. Then an explosive detonated and hit his friend's head. In that moment, Lawrence witnessed his first death as his friend breathed his last breath in my father's arms. The memory would never leave him. When recalling this story in later years, he would shift quickly from the difficult memory to a discussion of his next party or event with his Alpha Phi Alpha brothers.

Our family has always honored traditions. Serving in World War II, my father was following in the footsteps of other Malloys who had gone into combat. His ancestors Daniel and Archie

Malloy, along with many others, fought in the Civil War. His brother Braxton fought in World War I, and Leland also served in World War II. Members of the Malloy family often bragged loudly and proudly about their time at war.

The Black community was heavily involved in World War II, even as Jim Crow laws continued to restrict their lives at home: "More than one million African American men and women served in every branch of the U.S. armed forces during World War II. . . . This willingness on the part of African American soldiers to sacrifice their lives for a country that treated them as second-class citizens is remarkable. Various accounts relate how German prisoners of war could enter facilities reserved for white Americans that black servicemen could not patronize."[16]

Once the army released my father honorably, he had the funds through the GI Bill to make his way to medical school and become a doctor, like his brothers, uncles, cousins, and father. The medical field was a major challenge for Black people, given that the majority of medical schools were divisions of predominantly white colleges. Only a few colleges and universities were integrated, and applications from Black students were often denied in the forties.

Meharry and Howard University did offer medical programs and were popular in the Black community. Upon finishing medical school, most doctors of color had to start their own practices, but they were denied access to resources, equipment, and the various tools they needed. It took tenacity and determination as well as courage to combat the systemic racism in medicine as well as in the larger society.

The war ended in 1945, and the next year, Lawrence went off to study at Howard University, using the money he had saved from the Army and from working with his father. He also got a scholarship. Shortly after joining his sisters in Washington, DC, he went to a dance and met Loncie Norwood of Cleveland, Ohio, who was just turning eighteen. Lawrence was immediately smitten.

While Lawrence was in school, William was fighting to keep his land; white supremacist groups were watching to see if the land were to come available. High taxation and policies that allowed others to purchase land if the taxes were delinquent were part of the systemic practices that reduced land ownership in the Black community.

The inheritance of the land previously owned by William's deceased father, Daniel, in Laurel Hill was in question. As Black descendants, William and his siblings had to go by the book to be sure they received their inheritance; before Arthur passed away, they appointed William's brother J. R. Malloy to make the estate his focus. The form making J. R. the administrator of the estate was signed by William and his siblings Percy Malloy, Arthur Malloy, J. R. Malloy, and Mary Anne Brown. This allowed them to fend off any court cases that might come their way.

Though there were no sons left in Laurinburg to assist with W. M. Malloy and Son, William remained in town with his wife, Hattie, and her children. He became more deeply involved at Bowers Chapel, teaching Sunday school and attending all the Yadkin Eastern Sunday School Conventions. William remained firmly attached to the Laurinburg community. Nothing could separate him from his roots—nothing but the same groups that previously tried to attack the town.

10. COUNTRY TO TOWN

My father, much like his own father, loved his home. With Loncie, he created a love-filled home in the Maryland suburbs, adding a back porch that he built by hand. He never wanted my daughter or me to go too far away, but when LeeAnét was in her last year at Springbrook High School in Maryland, she decided to stray from the family legacy at Howard University and go to college in New York City. I understood her decision: As a young performer, she was captivated by the lights and charm of New York and wanted to be close to her Broadway dreams.

LeeAnét had spent her entire young life at Howard University, appearing in her first show at Cramton Auditorium on the campus at the age of two, directed by my professor LaVerne Reed. I also brought her to Howard with me when I returned to school. Mike Malone, one of the professors and renowned director and choreographer, would tease her: "Are you a student here yet?"

For her application to college in New York, she recorded monologues of material ranging from Shakespeare to Ntozake Shange's *For Colored Girls Who Have Considered Suicide / When the Rainbow Is Enuf*. LeeAnét received a competitive arts scholarship to college and left for New York City. Unfortunately, the school did not have any available housing. I made my way to New York City to find a job so I could support her journey and secure a place for her to stay while in school.

When she completed her first day, she noticed that she was one of only two Black people in her classes. There were no other people of color. She made the most of her time and loved the classes. She also started an internship with Danielides Communications, a public relations agency that represents clients such as Emmy Award–winning daytime drama star Susan Lucci. Her work excursions included trips to the Russian Tea Room, where she assisted at events, ate pancakes stuffed with caviar and sour cream, and chatted with President Bill Clinton's family.

All was well until one day in her first year. She was sitting in a circle in her theater history class when a fellow student referred to Black people as "colored." The other students scolded her instantly: "You can't call African Americans 'colored'!" An argument about the proper term for Black people ensued. The professor turned to my daughter, the only person of color in the class. She could only hear her own heartbeat as the teacher asked, "Well, LeeAnét, you are the only one here. What term should we use?" In that moment, she had to speak for an entire race.

That incident, coupled with being an "only" in most of her classes, left her utterly chagrined. She had been yearning to perform in the shows she saw me in as a child, and she wanted to study with Mike Malone, who had worked with Josephine Baker. All of this, coupled with the promise of a car from my father, prompted her to leave New York and transfer to Howard University.

My father was excited. Though he had retired from his position as postmaster at the university, he was still a very proud

Bison. LeeAnét had been raised in his household from the age of nine; he provided for her as if she were his child rather than grandchild.

When it was time for her to register, he walked the campus, making sure no stone was left unturned. He went to the administration building to get her in the system and to make sure everything was correct, then walked across campus to see Ms. Deneal in the Fine Arts Dean's office to make sure she knew his granddaughter was coming to the school. He even tried to adopt LeeAnét. If he had done so, LeeAnét would have been able to attend through the school's tuition remission program, which allowed children of employees to attend for free, as I did. Her academic scholarships, combined with assistance from my father and me, made it possible for her to attend Howard. He wanted her to have the advantages he knew were needed to succeed. LeeAnét still works with the university today.

The forties brought many advances for the Black community. President Franklin D. Roosevelt's 1941 Executive Order 8802 ending segregation in national defense jobs brought more employment opportunities. The same year, the Tuskegee Airmen became the first Black men to perform as aviators in the US Army. Lawrence kept his eyes on what was happening in the world, from politics to popular culture.

If my father wasn't listening to music, he would watch films in his spare time. He was a filmmaker as a hobby, fascinated with capturing memorable moments with his 8mm Revere camera. He could fix cameras, projectors, and recording devices and was a certified electrician, skills he learned back in Laurinburg working with his dad. He used to call himself a jack-of-all-trades and a master of one, never identifying that "one."

In 1939, he saw Hattie McDaniel win an Oscar for her role in *Gone with the Wind*. Seeing films that portrayed Black people only as servants and maids was discomforting given that he had grown up among Black business owners and entrepreneurs who hired their own service people.

Gradually, new figures were emerging in the fight for the rights of Black people. In 1945, James Farmer advocated for equal employment rights, and Adam Clayton Powell Jr. took office as the first Black congressman from New York. Leland witnessed this election firsthand as a New York resident. Jim Crow was still running amuck, but Lawrence saw Black people breaking new barriers, including in 1947 when Jackie Robinson joined the Brooklyn Dodgers baseball team.

Before making his way to Howard University, Lawrence sent money to his sister Dot in DC to help her purchase a home, which would give them all a secure place to live. A home was also a good investment in the future: "By even owning a house, you create equity, and that creates wealth for the next generation."[1] During my father's time at Howard, he stayed with Dot and her husband on Georgia Avenue within walking distance of the campus.

At the age of twenty-four, a few years older than his fellow students, Lawrence began his studies. Howard University provided a safe space isolated from the Jim Crow effects surrounding him and other Black men coming out of World War II. As Alexis Clark noted in *The New York Times*: "Black soldiers returning from the war found the same socioeconomic ills and racist violence that they faced before. Despite their sacrifices overseas, they still struggled to get hired for well-paying jobs."[2]

Clark quoted Charissa Threat, a history professor at Chapman University:

> AT THE HEART OF IT WAS A KIND of nervousness and fear that many whites had that returning Black veterans would upset the racial status quo.... They saw images of Black soldiers coming from abroad from places like Germany and England, where Black soldiers were intermingling with whites and had a lot more freedom.... During the war, the N.A.A.C.P. and other civil rights groups encouraged Blacks to enlist in the military so they could receive G.I. benefits. After the war, however, the bill failed to propel Black servicemen into the middle class in the numbers it did for white veterans.[3]

Nationwide, though the Black community served in the largest numbers in US history during World War II, the GI Bill was not inclusive and its promises did not manifest for Black veterans. As journalist Erin Blakemore stated, "Though the bill helped white Americans prosper and accumulate wealth in the postwar years, it didn't deliver on that promise for veterans of color. In fact, the wide disparity in the bill's implementation ended up helping drive growing gaps in wealth, education, and civil rights between white and Black Americans."[4]

On the home front, North Carolina had contributed to the war effort. During the war, Laurinburg's land became a resource for the country. The North Carolina Department of Natural and Cultural Resources notes, "On August 28, 1942, the U.S. Army activated Laurinburg-Maxton air base in Scotland County. The facility, where glider pilots trained, played a little-known role in the Allied victory in World War II."[5]

Though the soldiers fought with pride, the trauma of being at war left many with mental, emotional, and physical wounds. Just "moving on" might have seemed like a good idea, but with no therapy or comfort to weather the storms of trauma and discrimination veterans struggled to adjust to civilian life. Assuming they could do so with no repercussions was presumptuous.

My father was no exception. He recognized his triggers in daily life and never thought twice about them. He would have a panic attack at the sight of me getting in a car to leave the house, for example. When I lost a tooth, he broke into tears. A loud sound would transport him back to the war. He never mentioned having post-traumatic stress disorder, which was in fact unknown as a term then.

My father's exposure to trauma seemed a normal part of his life. It was something his father had experienced as well. William witnessed the insurrection in Laurinburg and saw burning crosses. My father was chased as a boy.

During my studies in music therapy at Howard University under Dr. Ara Thomas-Brown, I learned that post-traumatic stress was not acknowledged by the American Psychiatric Association as a disorder until 1980. PTSD has great effects on the emotional state of the individual and the mental health of immediate family members who witness and empathize with their pain. When triggered by everyday situations, victims repeat the initial trauma in their head and over-examine elements of daily life.

Before and even after the disorder is acknowledged, victims often self-medicate as they try not to relive the points of trauma—anything to stop the harsh, scary thoughts and intense escalation of emotions. Many suffer with these effects, thinking they are normal. As I learned more about the topic, I saw direct connections to my father's stories and the experiences I had with him.

But as a veteran in the summer of 1946, Lawrence walked the

campus of Howard University with a Southern charm and confidence that dripped off his tailored suits. He was still eager to follow in his brother's footsteps as a doctor. The environment at Howard wasn't new to him. My father grew up surrounded by Black thinkers, creatives, workers, and philosophers at Laurinburg Institute. What was new to him was city life. The energy of Washington, DC, was quicker, the homes were smaller, and the farms were miles away, owned mostly by white farmers. With President Harry S. Truman in the White House, my father imagined new doors opening.

Hailing from Cleveland, Ohio, Loncie L. Norwood, short in stature with curly hair and brown skin with orange reddish undertones, was in her second year as a music major on a singing scholarship. The eldest girl of eleven children, she walked the campus with similar confidence, but hers stemmed from knowing that she worked hard. She was the first in her family to attend a four-year college, and she felt the responsibility that came with it.

The staff at Howard included professors like Dr. Charles R. Drew, who revolutionized medicine with new techniques for blood storage. He served as the assistant director of the first American Red Cross Blood Bank and was chief surgeon and head of the surgery department at Freedmen's Hospital. Alain LeRoy Locke, who received his doctorate from Harvard University, was a notable philosopher on the progress of the Black community and its ability to resist and shift unfair treatment through new mindsets and behaviors. Another Harvard graduate, political science professor Dr. Ralph Bunche, would later become the first Black person to win the Nobel Prize. It was an exciting time to be at the university.

The legacy of W. M. Malloy and Son was now carried on by

Leland, who was working in construction in New York. Like Lawrence, Leland fought in World War II. He was forty-four years old when drafted from his new home at 305 Quincy Street in Brooklyn. William served as his point of contact on his draft card. After working as a carpenter for years in the city, he transitioned to working for WPW Construction in Brooklyn, New York.

Back in Laurinburg, William was living a life of leisure, smoking Cuban cigars and drinking iced tea with a splash of lemonade (known decades later as an Arnold Palmer) as he relaxed with Hattie on his pristine white porch. The books he perused on those lazy days ranged from the Bible to novels such as Zora Neale Hurston's *Their Eyes Were Watching God* and Richard Wright's *Native Son*. He also read *Mary Chesnut's Diary*, a personal account of the Civil War. This book included a mention of the Malloy family: The author refers to her musician friend "Mr. Mallory" from North Carolina. My father spoke often of the book; though Mary Chesnut was a Confederate, he wanted to read about the history of the town.

Zelda and the children of Hattie, the last of William's children in Laurinburg, would join them for discussions and tea on the expansive porch, which was flanked by pillars. The house parties were now relegated to times when all the children, now adults, came home. When Braxton, Leland, Emmett, Dot, Mae, Grace, or Lawrence visited, dinner was prepared, and neighbors joined them for the breaking of bread. *The New York Age* articles chronicling such visits had tapered off in the thirties, and *The Africo-American Presbyterian*, which had kept up with the happenings of the Malloy family, had ended its run in 1938.[6]

Sometimes William put his carpentry hat back on and assisted with repairs in the home of a neighbor in need. When Bowers Chapel needed repairs, he was there to make sure the work he had put in over the years remained intact. He was also on call after tornadoes hit. In a photo dated August 29, 1940, a group of Black residents in Laurinburg look at several homes that had been ripped to shreds after an F1 tornado hit, with winds as high as 112 miles per hour.[7] No matter how well homes were prepared, these violent storms always resulted in displaced families and repair work for William and other Black construction workers.

Though William and Hattie were married and spent much time together, they kept separate homes. It was uncommon for Black families in the forties to have multiple homes, but with their combined business acumen, they knew to hold on to their various properties. "William and his third wife got married but didn't live together," my cousin Wilbur told me. "William lived with his eldest daughter Zelda." The other children were in DC, Massillon, and Brooklyn after William's third marriage.

One of the ways the Malloy family held it together and stayed connected was by throwing parties at 740 Newton Place in DC, Dot's house. Lawrence invited all of his friends at the university. It was a good time to laugh and joke with one another. These gatherings were much like the parties at the White House on the Hill in Laurinburg.

They all found comfort in being with family. Dot, Grace, and Lawrence were all living in DC, six to seven hours away by car from their assets and land in Laurinburg. William had set them all up for success by maintaining several homes and pieces of land there in the family name. In a world that could be both expensive and dangerous, with difficult roadblocks for Black people, these properties were a great asset.

The roadblocks were very real. According to the Federal Reserve History website, "The FHA [Federal Housing Administration] began redlining at the very beginning of its operations in 1934, as FHA staff concluded that no loan could be economically sound if the property was located in a neighborhood that was or could become populated by Black people, as property values might decline over the life of the 15- to 20-year loans."[8]

Given systemic blocks like redlining, William's land in the family name created paths to generational wealth. My father also knew that beyond his good looks, charm, and pressed suits, the real estate holdings made him a good catch, and he was ready to explore. Meanwhile my mother, Loncie, knew there was a running joke that if you don't meet your mate in college, you can't expect to meet him or her later.

Loncie was on the other side of the Howard campus when she heard about a party at Dot's house from her best friend Modise, her soror from Sigma Gamma Rho. She was in her Slowe Hall dormitory and had to be convinced to join the crowd after hearing that a nice group of men from the medical school would be there.

As Loncie entered Dot's row house, she noticed a handsome man. As she prepared to walk past him, he turned and looked down at her and said, "Who are you? Have I seen you before?"

They struck up a conversation. He told her to stay right where she was, not to move. Loncie thought this was quite funny. Inquisitive about this dapper man, she stood there until he got back.

When Lawrence returned, he couldn't believe she had waited.

Neither could she. But something ignited between them at that first encounter, and soon they were inseparable. Lawrence told Loncie that he knew what he wanted and need not look any further for a girlfriend. Loncie was progressive, with a lightning quickness. She was a sharp thinker and had amazing social skills. Her wit provided needed joy.

Lawrence's dating etiquette followed Southern ways and traditions, much like his father's. He and Loncie met at Dot's house to go on picnics, lunch dates, and movie excursions where Lena Horne lit up the screen. Though Lawrence followed the courting rituals of a college man, as the youngest Malloy, he figured he would remain single much longer. Loncie, on the other hand, knew she wanted to marry him.

Lawrence let her know that he wasn't the marrying type. She decided to buy herself a ring but didn't mention where it came from. After Lawrence took notice, the thought of someone else with Loncie sent him down on one knee to propose.

During the summer break, he brought her to Laurinburg to meet the family: his daddy, Aunt Zelda, and his stepmother Hattie and her children, including Thelma and Dess, to whom he had become close. Lawrence took Loncie to show her off to his family and to show his family to Loncie; both sides were impressed. It had been a long while since Loncie's girlhood in Georgia, and after growing up in Cleveland, this new connection to Southern life was very appealing. It allowed her to see how Lawrence had been raised and how his father had focused on bringing up God-fearing children.

The White House on the Hill was as pristine inside as it was outside. They broke bread together at the dining room table with a meal prepared by Zelda, then gathered for tea and a few spirits in the living room. The men went out to the backyard to puff on their cigars while the ladies gathered on the porch looking over the lawn. Laurinburg was a great place to fall further in love.

Within one year of dating and meeting each other's families, Lawrence and Loncie were married. Still at Howard University, they focused on finishing their undergraduate degrees. Loncie wasn't a full-time student, as her scholarship included an entry-level job as a secretary in the US Department of Health, Education, and Welfare. She moved into Newton Place with Lawrence, Dot, and Oliver, as it was near campus.

In 1948, a year after their wedding, Lawrence also took a job with the federal government, working as a postal field service worker as a grade PFS-4 (Postal Field Service grade 4) and window clerk, which extended the time it took him to get his undergraduate degree.

Though the university was a safe environment, when major national events took place that affected Black people, Howard was bustling with energy. In 1948, President Truman desegregated the military. Military service would be a much different experience for future Malloys who fought for their country.

That same year, Lawrence's dear friend Dizzy Gillespie, who was world-renowned at that point, was hit by a car while riding his bicycle. The accident affected his playing, particularly his ability to reach high notes. He sued, but he was informed that because he was already wealthy, he could only be awarded a thousand dollars by the court.

For the Malloys, everything was about generational wealth, and Lawrence was eager to build his own. He was diligent in balancing his bank account and maintaining his land. He wanted to make sure Loncie had the luxuries of life, such as traveling and shopping, and he also enjoyed nice suits.

Loncie's family, wanting to check in on their fancy daughter and her new wealthy husband, came to visit DC from Cleveland. Loncie made sure the house was pristine. This was a big trip for her mother and stepfather, Helena and Charles Haley, and her younger sister Prunella Norwood (later Prunella Kinds). Lawrence wanted to impress them as well, since he had only met them a few times.

The Wilson Line was a luxury excursion steamboat company that offered daily trips between Washington, DC, and Mount Vernon, VA, and other points of interest. Lawrence and Loncie had been waiting for an occasion to take a boat trip, and this was it. As they drove along the streets of their city, the couple pointed out the buildings where they worked. The group arrived at the dock in Washington, DC, dressed in their Sunday best and joined the line to board the grandiose steamboat, which was heading to Mount Vernon, the home of George Washington.[9]

An attendant for the Wilson Line refused to let them board due to their race. The family spoke up instantly in a flurry of emotions and frustration, stating that this discrimination was illegal. They went promptly to the office on site, where an official informed them that the attendant was supposed to allow them on board.[10]

When they returned, they were refused a second time. They went to the office again, and this time they were told that the attendant *was* following company policy by not allowing "colored people" to board. Lawrence let them know that the family would be taking them to court. The company representatives were not concerned.

The family returned to Dot's house and began to discuss their case and organize. Lawrence was upset but found relief in the family working together, with the women leading the charge. The case was underway.

Loncie graduated in May 1951, while Lawrence continued his

studies to become a doctor. At her graduation, Loncie was five months' pregnant with their first child. In September 1951, she gave birth to a son. Life was looking up.

A few months later, the verdict on their lawsuit was released to the press: "The Wilson Lines . . . has been ordered by the Interstate Commerce Commission to discontinue its policy of catering to white patrons only. The ICC order came on as a complaint filed by Mrs. Helena Haley, Charles Haley, Loncie Malloy and Prunella Norwood . . . who sought to purchase tickets and were refused on Sept. 15 1950."[11] They won the case.

However, though the boat company was forced to change its policy, the family was denied the ten thousand dollars in damages they sought in compensation for their humiliation. The commission stated: "It was held that since nobody but those seeking the tickets and the ticket agent knew of the transaction according to the commission's interpretation of the evidence presented, there was no basis for the allegation of humiliation."[12]

Seventy-five years later, this case is still the talk of the family. Everyone involved knew they made a change for the betterment of the community. At the same time, they were wrongfully denied damages but had no recourse. The Wilson Line continued on and became a larger conglomerate before being liquidated. Though not entirely satisfied with the outcome of the case, my parents had to keep moving forward since they had a newborn son.

My father had a love of politics and history, and his new job at the postal service was fascinating to him given the technical work with numbers and the impact of the service on others. It helped to fill the void he felt leaving his father's company, which provided for the Laurinburg community.

Lawrence did well in the School of Medicine at Howard University until one fateful day. While learning about plasma in a class, a cascade of emotions he hadn't felt before enveloped him. He felt the room shake, though there was no earthquake. His breath became heavy, and the beating of his heart was amplified in his ears. The sight of the blood took him right back to the field in Paris where he held his dying buddy, and he passed out. The ringing of the noonday bell shifted him out of his post-traumatic trance. He knew then the medical field was not for him. There was no way to push through such an experience. Trauma-induced hemophobia was the formal diagnosis my father never received. But his fear of blood would become a blessing in disguise, allowing him to try things he might have never pursued.

By 1952, Lawrence had earned over two hundred credit hours studying English, French, pre-law, education, physics, mathematics, sociology, philosophy, humanities, and history, which became his major. He graduated that year with a bachelor's degree.

My parents pooled their money and received assistance from the GI Bill, enabling them to purchase a row house on Ames Street, a few miles from Dot's similar house and Howard University. The house was humble, with two stories and a partially paved backyard with a patch of grass, just big enough to sit outside with friends and grill or have a cigar. The community was segregated in DC's Northeast area, and the young couple quickly became friends with their neighbors.

Many had young children, and everyone looked out for one another. If you needed some sugar or to make an emergency phone call, you could go right next door on either side of the house. Loncie and Lawrence were proud to have their name on their first mortgage. Lawrence was happy to be in a community whose members supported one another. It was similar to Laurinburg, but with less grass.

Back in North Carolina, William was battling health concerns. Hypertension was starting to get the best of him as he neared ninety years old. In the cold of October 1953, Loncie and Lawrence traveled to Laurinburg with their two-year-old son so William could meet his grandson.

My grandfather was spending most of his time with his daughter Zelda, who was now married to Houchin, the only name we know him by. They all lived at 218 Dickson in Stewartsville Township in Scotland County. Loncie was happy to be back in Laurinburg, though she knew this might be the last time she would see her father-in-law. She had become fond of him.

Lawrence's siblings—Dot, Grace, Fairley Mae, Leland, Braxton, and Emmett—and their spouses were in and out of the house visiting William as well. William's legs were swollen, and he was in a chair when he met his grandson. He was no longer the tall and commanding man he had been, but he smiled and joked, still exhibiting the Malloy spirit and vibrant energy. Everyone took photos to save the moment and broke bread as always.

A few months later, days after Christmas, Zelda found her father dead in their home. His death certificate reported that he passed away from vascular insufficiency due to hypertension. He was in his late eighties, at a time when the life expectancy for all men, Black and white, was sixty-five. William died in the town he loved and never left.

11. GOING BACK TO MOVE FORWARD

Grieving, or rather pushing through grief, was a normal part of my father's life. For every death he experienced after the war, Lawrence released loud tears. For a few minutes, each drop had its own note, accented by a groan or moan. Then he would give out a hearty cry and let it go. When I was an adult, he told me he could no longer attend funerals because it was too much on his blood pressure.

A photo or a childhood story involving his father could send him into a spell, and he would chant, "I miss my daddy. He was the best man." On one occasion, I left a photo album open. When my father picked it up, he noticed William standing tall with a stern and dignified look.

His mood changed in an instant. After smiling, tears poured from his eyes. William taught Lawrence who he was, with help from the Bible, his sisters, and life experiences. Within his Laurinburg community and home, he was inundated by Black excellence. As he declared in his self-published booklet, he was born a colored man and would later become the first Black man in most of the federal government offices he worked in.

LAURETTA MALLOY NOBLE AND LEEANÉT NOBLE

The term *colored* was used in advertisements for Black businesses in Laurinburg, whose owners referred to themselves as colored and later Negro, reflecting these shifts in society. "Between the Civil War and World War II, the United States underwent a profound process of racial reorganization," write Harvard professors Jennifer L. Hochschild and Brenna M. Powell. "Officially recognized group categories expanded and contracted; socially recognized boundaries between groups blurred and shifted; citizens and public actors passionately debated who belonged in which group. Basic components of the racial order were revised, revisited, and fundamentally altered."[1]

In 1934, the year William and Hattie were married, they were both listed as "colored" on the marriage record, and Hattie's birth year was given as "about 1887." Dates were not clear because Black people didn't have birth certificates for many decades.

As a baby, Lawrence was listed as "Mulatto," as a young boy as "Colored," and as a tween as "Negro (Black)" with the last name of "Molloy." As a man in his early twenties, he was still listed as "Negro (Black)," and the family name was spelled "Malloy." In his thirties, Lawrence began calling himself a Black man, and in 1953 he was working in majority white spaces in the government.

Lincoln Heights High School, the first public high school for Black children in Scotland County, opened its doors in 1953, the year William died. Lincoln Heights gave Black students in Scotland County another option besides Laurinburg Institute for education beyond middle school. The board of education hired I. Ellis Johnson, a Laurinburg Institute teacher, as its first principal. Johnson, a member of the McDuffie family that led Laurinburg Institute, was a graduate of Snow Hill Normal and

Industrial Institute of Alabama. Lincoln Heights High School would later be renamed in his honor.

The Laurinburg Exchange reported in 2015 that there was tension between the Black teachers in both schools in the early days: "When Scotland County schools became integrated, the Black employees were told not to associate with staff from the Laurinburg Institute. He [Frank 'Bishop' McDuffie] said the state of NC was upset that the McDuffies wouldn't sell the land that housed the Laurinburg Institute. But Johnson was family and McDuffie said their relationship didn't change."[2]

Imagine if Walter P. Evans had never reached out to Booker T. Washington after the insurrection to establish Laurinburg Institute. Black students would have had no option for education that could lead to college from 1898 to 1953! This mighty Black community in the swamp town knew how to care for and sustain its own, and their work was not in vain, as shown by the success of the Black children who witnessed the community build and rebuild itself throughout their lives.

William's death created a void in my father's life: He had no Black male shoulder to lean on as he was navigating adulthood. His older brothers were not home during his youth. The Malloy men were taught to stand tall on their own feet.

William, knowing the importance of legacy, left his children the property he owned separately from Hattie, his third wife. The children were willed the house on Dixon Street and other properties. Braxton, Leland, Zelda, Emmett, Dot, Fairley Mae, Grace, and Lawrence did what seems to be impossible today: They divided the land evenly and created a family plan to manage it. There were no fights or disputes over the Laurinburg estate at the time.

Lawrence now owned land in his hometown. He knew this

would come to pass, but having the deed in his name allowed him to stand even taller. He vowed to keep this land for as long as he was alive and hoped his children would be able to do the same.

From their new home on Ames Street in Washington, DC, my parents, both driven to excel, kept pushing forward but with different objectives. Loncie wanted to be in a position to support her family as needed and to be able to visit Cleveland at her leisure, while Lawrence focused on upholding the family name and legacy.

Loncie found support in the arms of Lawrence. She took her responsibilities as an older sister in her family seriously and was focused on progressing in her career and bringing her dreams to life. She acknowledged that she sometimes needed to feel taken care of. And she, in turn, supported Lawrence.

When Lawrence would wake up in hot sweats from a post-traumatic stress episode within a dream, the therapeutic waves of Loncie's voice and songs released endorphins that calmed his anxiety. Her ability to calm him was an extra bonus in their relationship. They worked to keep their love sacred by attending church regularly, praying together, dancing together, and functioning as a unit with their son in tow.

They introduced each other proudly, saying, "This is my husband" or "This is my wife." They pushed hard in their careers to keep a lifestyle that reflected their vision as their family got bigger.

In her thirties, Loncie gave birth to me, her second and last child, and named me Lauretta Annette. I was told many times throughout my life that, like my brother, I was born by C-section. After my birth, Lawrence applied for a raise and was given the position of editorial assistant in the US Postal Service.

One year after that promotion, he became the editor of printed media, including a 75,000-copy weekly publication, the *Postal Bulletin*. When I was just three years old and my brother thirteen, we moved to Maryland.

Between 1948 and 1964, Lawrence went from a GS-7 to a GS-12 and was the editor of the national zip code directory and postal regulations. Though he shaped the zip codes for many areas, it was a work-for-hire position for which he did not get public credit. To receive recognition, he would add "architect of zip codes" to his walking résumé.

Our model home had a front and backyard, wildlife, and enough fertile land to plant vegetables and herbs. One year after integrating our Maryland neighborhood, in 1965 Lawrence received a promotion to grade PS-14 (Postal Service) making $17,800 a year (the equivalent of $175,359 in 2024). The median income in 1965 was about $6,900.[3] With Loncie's government salary, my parents were able to get involved in philanthropic efforts with local organizations and put their children in prestigious social organizations for youth.

In 1960, the government of Laurinburg created a twenty-year plan to improve the town. The goal of the Public Improvement Program was to "develop a capital budget for the city." The municipal budget exceeded eight hundred thousand dollars a year.[4] Proposed improvements included new tennis courts, road paving, power sources, land for new schools, and upgrades to Bizzell Street. Improvements in the Black community were less lavish and expansive. The "colored" community building slated for 1965 was to be located on a playground and would have no adult meeting space, unlike the white community building.[5] The separate but not equal way of society was sticking.

Other priorities included purchasing ten acres of land for a new Negro cemetery. Within the document, the words *Colored* and *Negro* were both used.[6] It is theorized that *Colored* included the large Native American communities that remained in Laurinburg.

The plan also proposed purchasing about fifteen acres for the site of a Negro elementary school in East Laurinburg in 1969 and the building of a Negro elementary school in East Laurinburg in 1970. Of course, many of these plans were derailed by school integration as Supreme Court cases and activism continued to aid in the stalled desegregation of North Carolina.

Many Black elders from Laurinburg believe that integration brought the downfall of many self-sustaining Black neighborhoods, as crime rates increased and businesses faltered. Others approved of integration efforts. In his book *The Color of Law*, Richard Rothstein writes, "Surveys show that most African Americans prefer integrated neighborhoods. So do whites. But African Americans define an integrated community as one in which from 20 to 50 percent of residents are African American. Whites define it as one where they dominate—and in which only 10 percent of residents are African American. When a neighborhood exceeds an African American presence of more than 10 percent, whites typically start to leave."[7]

In Laurinburg, the communities were evaluated by section; each one received different attention from the government in the sixties. The term *blight* was often used to describe areas suffering from a lack of resources, unevenly paved roads, no new houses, increased crime rates, and abandoned properties.

Laurinburg's July 1967 analysis gathered intel.[8] Though William had passed away, other elders remained who had held on to their homes, knowing the importance of legacy and of Laurinburg as a community. However, the reports were generalized, gathering bulk information from census reports. If a neighborhood was labeled as being full of "blight," it would receive limited resources.

While the northern side of Laurinburg, where Laurinburg Institute was located, and the area off of Stewartsville, where the majority of the Black community resided, suffered the loss of seventeen houses from fires in 1966, the community planned as many as twenty-eight new houses in areas that were majority white.

The 1967 analysis states, "It should be noted that, for the most part, new residential construction did not occur in areas with substandard housing. This is in part an indication that builders fear the spread of blight in such areas." The area where William last resided in Stewartsville had 918 non-white citizens.

One ordinary day when I was ten, while playing with Lady (our cocker spaniel–Lab mix, who was like my sibling), I was rushing to handle a matter between my Diahann Carroll "Julia" doll and her friend Skipper. I stopped cold in my tracks on my way to the dollhouse and stood staring at my father, who was on the phone without his customary smile. All I knew was that he was speaking with Aunt Dess. When a family member phoned from out of town, my brother and I were required to join the call one at a time to say hello.

After our hellos, my father continued with the call, responding, "Mmm," "Well, I'll be," and "I hear ya." Once he hung up the new push-button phone with its twelve fancy keys, my father looked at me standing there.

"What's wrong?" I asked.

"Daddy's house burned down."

I panicked, thinking he was speaking about himself, and yelled, "Oh, no, what do we do!"

When he saw my rising panic, he quickly forgot his emotions and instead tended to mine. "Don't worry, baby, everything is okay."

Then my father walked to the television, flicked it on, and sat back down. Laurinburg would never be the same for him now that his childhood house was gone, along with his father. I would never learn the cause of the fire. And my father had to let go of it in order to move forward.

In 1960, the population of Laurinburg was 8,242, with 3,140 non-white people making up 38.1 percent. From 1950 to 1960, the number of homes increased by 19.6 percent, but according to the neighborhood analysis of 1967, only 289 of the 1,179 homeowners were non-white. The city reports do not break down the ethnicities in the tallies. Rather, everyone is classified as white or non-white.

The population makeup of the sixties reflected a shift from the Black communities of homeowners and farm owners that my father and grandfather experienced. A lack of jobs, intimidation by white supremacist groups, and restrictive Jim Crow laws all had an impact on the exodus from Laurinburg. Everyone was impacted by this transformation: There were now 847 Black and white residents living in poverty, and the median income of the town was $3,558.

The entrepreneurial enterprises that populated Main Street in its prime, where Black and white patrons shopped, were ghosts of the past. Where was the next Booker T. Washington or W. E. B. Du Bois to encourage change in the South?

Du Bois continued to fight against discrimination through the NAACP and in books, newspapers, teachings, and conferences. He faced backlash, court cases, and more. He joined the Communist Party in 1961, and at the age of ninety-three moved to Ghana to continue his work until his death two years later,[9] on the eve of the March on Washington for Jobs and Freedom.

In Laurinburg, Lawrence had learned resistance through education and building rather than protesting racism and systemic disenfranchisement. The sixties were a new era of bold steps, and the March on Washington made waves. Lawrence started funneling funds back into his education and returned to school, studying agriculture, editing, and writing at George Washington University, and he took courses in writing and management at Oberlin College in Ohio.

Dr. Martin Luther King Jr.'s assassination in 1968 deeply affected my father. The murder was a huge factor in his decision to apply at the family alma mater, Howard University, after his job was abolished. It was time to serve the community the way his own father had and to take his education to the next generation of Black thinkers. The area around Howard's campus looked very different, as many businesses had been burned down in the riots following MLK's assassination.

My family's visits to Laurinburg from DC continued. Lawrence needed to check on his land and to visit Zelda, who remained in her home with her husband. Lawrence made sure his children and Loncie had as many opportunities as possible to see the town and school that were so dear to him.

In 1957, Sam Jones, a Laurinburg Institute graduate, joined the NBA. The school was developing a reputation in professional basketball with players who attracted attention outside of traditional education. The school's budding reputation in sports was appealing to the town as a whole, since people from all backgrounds love sports and bragging about hometown heroes. This was a shift. Though his father's home was no longer there, Lawrence realized that the spirit of the Laurinburg he knew was something he could not leave behind.

Another major shift in the town came with integration in the sixties. "Scotland County was home to several African-American schools, an African-American boarding school, a Native American school and segregated white schools that came together in 1969 to form one integrated school system," *The Laurinburg Exchange* reported.[10] This occurred long after the 1954 Supreme Court ruling in *Brown v. Board of Education*.

Frank "Bishop" McDuffie, the current president and third-generation leader of Laurinburg Institute, observed that areas like Bizzell Street (called Brazil Street by some Southern natives) had been buzzing with Black businesses since 1903. But the district fizzled with the onset of integration, as many stopped patronizing the businesses as frequently.

Writing in *The Laurinburg Exchange* in 2015, Scott Witten spoke on efforts from locals to restore some of Bizzell Street's Black landmarks, specifically Central Hotel: "Built in 1893, the two-story brick building is the oldest building in downtown Laurinburg's historic district. First known as the Central Hotel and later Hotel Dixie, its proximity to the railroad greeted passenger trains arriving from Wilmington or points farther inland. It also served the African-American community as a hotel and boarding house through the first half of the 20th century and from 1959 until 1997 was the location of a series of popular restaurants." Witten spoke with John Goodwin, an art collector looking to restore the hotel, who stated, "This particular place is important and we should respect it, love it and admire it as much as any other part of town." He said, "It definitely has significance to me. It was the first building where African-Americans could rent a space."[11]

Our family also owned businesses on Bizzell Street, including laundromats and restaurants. The Black-owned businesses on Bizzell Street faded in and out in the 1960s—the fate of many wealthy and prosperous Black communities before and after Tulsa's prosperous Greenwood district was burned to the ground in 1921.

A seldom-told story about William Alexander Leidesdorff, a mixed-race man, illustrates the fate of numerous wealthy Black people in Laurinburg. A ship's commander, he invested his money in imports and exports and expanded his real estate portfolio to include hotels in the 1840s. He lived in a lavish mansion in San Francisco and was well-off. When gold was discovered near his home, his assets were worth over a million dollars. In 1848, he passed away in his sleep.

In *Black Fortunes*, Shomari Wills describes what happened next: "A real estate investor . . . found Leidesdorff's estranged mother . . . his sole known heir. He convinced her to sign over her son's property for a payment of $75,000 ($2.1 million). The Leidesdorff estate was worth more than $1.4 million ($38 million). With the stroke of a pen, the fortune and legacy of America's first black millionaire was stolen."[12]

A similar story appears in an article and video by Arpita

Aneja and Olivia B. Waxman that charts the rise and fall of numerous Black Wall Street towns such as the Jackson Ward of Richmond, Virginia, established in 1871. The town declined after 1940 and into the sixties, when the population was decimated by redlining and a flight of people leaving for what seemed to be better opportunities elsewhere.[13]

Today, parts of Laurinburg's story remain to be told. Wealthy Black families of doctors and entrepreneurs such as the Malloys, changemakers and rich business owners such as Walter P. Evans, and tennis champions such as Nathaniel Jackson are all relatively unknown. In 2024, the town had one of the highest poverty rates in North Carolina and was plagued by storm-damaged buildings and a dwindling population. You might think a community like the one Lawrence grew up in never existed.

Many have gotten stuck in an echo chamber when it comes to Black history. The Global Fund for Children, a nonprofit that focuses on creating better lives for children, observes: "Information can come from many different sources and perspectives. But when you're only hearing the same perspectives and opinions over and over again, you may be in something called an echo chamber."[14] An echo chamber can skew perspectives and alter facts, especially when the facts you know are altered from the start. When we don't know the accomplishments of the past, we risk limiting our future.

How can we combat this? "Make a habit of checking multiple news sources to ensure you're getting complete, objective info," the organization suggests. "Interact with people of different perspectives, and take care to discuss new ideas with facts, patience, and respect. Remember that just because you want something to be true, doesn't make it fact."[15]

When people stand up only for their own partial understanding of a subject and declare war on opposing opinions, they are in essence saying, "The baby goes out with the bathwater." This mentality fails to acknowledge that all of us are in the same tub.

Psychology's quest to heal emotionally bewildered people implements strategies to help the harmed expel all of their thoughts, unpacking them over time before the patients can move on to higher-functioning pursuits of happiness. But when it comes to people of color whose ancestors were violently oppressed for generations, just think how many people who needed to emote and unpack their psychological, physical, and sexual trauma have passed down DNA markers of stress, as epigenetics shows us.

Historically, data and census information has been manipulated or selectively presented to support specific viewpoints. In the nineteenth century, the US census underwent changes to improve accuracy; but even then, the way data was collected and reported could have been influenced by bias. But we are still grateful; without the census reports, our information about our ancestors would be further limited. It's important to have diverse groups contributing to discussions and solutions rather than relying on a single perspective.

I knew I had to write this book. I also had to listen to my father, even if it meant going back to my childhood.

My father made career strides after leaving Laurinburg, but it was because of Laurinburg and his family that he had the drive and support to do so. I wasn't the first generation of my family to attend college; I was the third.

My father was the last of his blood-related siblings to go to college. He and my mother spoke fluent French and continued their education after receiving their undergraduate degrees. Living up to their accomplishments was daunting to my brother and me, but they inspired us nevertheless.

It was in Laurinburg where my grandfather's business was supported by the community, a community that came together and cleared the land for the first Black boarding school in the nation. They did it with their bare hands. White allies connected with Black community leaders to help get Black leaders on the school board and to start Black schools during Reconstruction. Their camaraderie was strong.

Black and white allies formed a new party that angered supremacist groups, who stirred a torture campaign in towns that were prospering. That prosperity ignited a brutal insurrection. Amid these trials, the community came together and walked tall, starting businesses that served everyone, no matter their race.

Southern pride in the swamp town of Laurinburg was strong and intertwined with Black excellence as we know it today. During enslavement on the large North Carolina plantations, individuals and families created strategic systems to live by and to escape from. They created coded songs, languages, and customs; found moments of joy; and crafted plans to escape. After enslavement, the newly free and those who were born free went back to their African roots by creating self-sustaining businesses and communities.

As far back as 1559, in places like Senegal and Gambia, the Fula people created well-organized towns. The community of Laurinburg had its own evolving character, economy, and culture. The town's connection to Scotland became official in 1993 when Oban became its sister city. Papers such as *The Laurinburg*

Exchange share vital stories of Black history in the community. Everyone came together to fight the devastating storms, a force with no opposing sides, and all attended the annual Highland Games, enjoyed by people of all backgrounds.

Stories about towns like Laurinburg fill in the deliberate gaps in Black history. They live in between the lines and references, taking space solely in the hearts and minds of our elders, who are now generations away from the source.

We have to connect to our oral West African griot histories. Because I still have unresolved questions, my research restarts daily. Looking for information about how Uncle Leland died, I discovered that my great-grandfather passed away during a pre-insurrection riot that claimed to have no fatalities.

In my research, I stumbled on a ripped and torn yellow-stained newspaper that chronicled the wealthy and prosperous lives of Black people in Laurinburg in the early twentieth century. Other documents from this era all claimed they were poor and downtrodden. I knew the truth not only from my father's stories, but also by the way he carried himself and the messages I found in books, street names, and churches.

In recent years, I have visited Laurinburg with my daughter and driven down the streets of boarded-up and empty homes. My father's stories painted a picture of a town that was no longer there. But in my mind, my father's Laurinburg was alive.

Now, we had the information to see beyond our eyes and share his memories. I had to go back to my childhood. I had to listen again to tell the true story as my daughter and I wrote together.

"Good *night* in the mornin'," Daddy would yell out with an extra emphasis on the word *night*, like a jazz scat. I would look at him, staring, trying to understand his outburst. This was not new: Watching my father was always entertaining. He used this phrase when upset, as well as when he was happy or surprised.

At that moment he was looking at one of the photo albums I had propped open and forgot to close. I was excited about creating a football game in the living room with my big brother's equipment while he was at basketball practice.

The photos dated back to the 1920s. They were kept in such good condition that the images looked new.

My father didn't look at them much, but when he did, his expressions erupted in uncontained joy. In so many ways, he never left the Laurinburg he knew. He kept the land his entire life and took it wherever he went. If you knew my father, you knew Laurinburg.

My father shared the joys of his town every chance he could, and my daughter and I were listening, even when we weren't. Now we are his walking résumés.

Postscript

THE SPIRIT PREVAILS

My brother, Leon, was known for working as the chief negotiator for the local government in Washington, DC, and as a criminal defense investigator for the federal courts in the eighties and nineties. He often spoke about the process of researching and investigating and following leads, no matter what seemed obvious. His words stuck with me during this process, as the information I was seeking was far from the surface. For example, I uncovered Charles Malloy's mistress's name *eleven years* into my research.

I knew it was vital for me to share this process with my daughter. We often work together as performers, producers, and writers. Our collaboration was especially easy when this investigation started to shape up as a mystery with missing relatives, wars, and more. I learned she had a special relationship with my father, writing school papers about the family after interviewing him and gathering intel on his journey. We cannot continue the legacy of the family or the town without sharing it with the next generation. And now I'll pass the pen to my daughter, LeeAnét.

Beyond being a child performer and playing with my imaginary friends, I found that growing up with my grandfather Lawrence was an adventure of its own. His stories were as enthralling as the Shakespearean dramas I grew up reading and work on today. I heard them so often as a child and teenager that, at times, I took them for granted, eager to play a video game or talk with friends on the phone instead.

As an adult, I found that his stories were embedded in my subconscious. I never felt limited in life, due not only to the accomplishments of my family but also to how they navigated the world with an ingrained confidence.

My grandmother Loncie spoke my name as if it belonged to royalty, holding her head up and using a bit of her fluent French for added flare. I went with her to philanthropic meetings in Montgomery County, Maryland, where members strategized ways to navigate systemic racism through programs, court cases, and other means.

I walked the campus of Howard University with my grandfather on many occasions. The joy that flowed through him as he walked made me stand a little taller.

Given that my grandfather was older than most of my peers' elders, I could see that his days of traveling out of state had passed. Until I was about eight years old, I visited Laurinburg only through his stories, using my imagination and his words to draw a landscape of this prominent Black community.

When my mother took me to Laurinburg for the first time, we shared the driving—a six-hour drive was long for both of us. I was excited to see my grandfather's home. He and my mother had made sure I had everything I needed growing up. Even today, his passing, as well as the loss of my grandmother when I was six, brings waves of grief. When I look back on my time with them, listening, processing, and celebrating the connection, the mourning is coupled with beautiful memories and grateful breaths. Seeing Laurinburg with my own two eyes furthered my connection with them in a spiritual way.

As my mother and I rode through Laurinburg's narrow streets, we rolled down the windows of the car just enough to feel the breeze flowing from the water and rippling the beautiful cypress trees. We gave ourselves a tour of the town following the directions from my grandfather's stories.

We rode down streets bearing the family name and saw the historical Stewart-Hawley-Malloy House and a diverse community of houses named Malloy Woods. As we continued down the narrow roads, we viewed numerous plots of empty land. I began to dream of what could be built in those spaces: wellness centers, tiny homes, a performing arts center, health food stores, and more.

We drove down Bizzell Street, now a dusty road with vacant buildings of all sizes and a yet-to-be-remodeled hotel. We drove to historical markers of the mills that had our last name on them. When we could, we jumped out of the car, leaving it parked on the side of the road, and took pictures posing by the family name for social media. We were proud to belong there, because it had been our family's hometown for generations.

We encountered a number of streets named after one Malloy or another. The race of the people honored on those street signs did not matter. They were still a part of our bloodline. We saw facilities that spoke out to us in memory of places my mother visited as a child with the family. I felt like I was riding through a time capsule.

But once I left the imaginative world conjured up by my grandfather, I felt the reality of the town's current state close in on me.

Where were the plaques honoring the Black people in my family who had contributed to the town's history? Where were the markers, the memories of the town, to be seen by the next generations?

Then we traveled within the twelve square miles of the city to the hallowed brick buildings of McGirt's Bridge Road, where Laurinburg Institute once bustled with energy from young people eager to learn and to play in vibrant basketball games.

We saw a lone man on the street. He was wearing a three-piece suit, perhaps his Sunday best in preparation for church. We pulled over and asked him for directions to my great-grandfather's house. With a slow Southern drawl and a bright smile, he waved his arms to show us each turn we needed to make. His visuals allowed us to easily navigate to William's house, the one he built for Aunt Dess. My mother remarked that it looked shockingly smaller, similar to when we visited our home in Maryland many years after we lived there. The Laurinburg homestead was over one hundred years old and didn't appear to have been painted in years.

Looking into the window, I envisioned my grandfather's sisters sitting in the front room, reading by the fireplace. Those images shifted as I noticed the furniture belonging to the current family. My thoughts moved to how the walls he built housed generations of Laurinburg residents who most likely didn't know his name.

This bothered me, but the surroundings eased my anxiety. It was as if God were holding a microphone to the large trees, birds, creeks, and crickets that surrounded us. I looked around and tried to envision what the area was like in the nineteenth and early twentieth centuries, when there were no paved roads. What were the police like? The town's officials? Did they greet everyone as they strolled the streets on foot and horseback? What were their thoughts on this town? And why was this place at a standstill now, empty except for a lone man in a three-piece suit?

With such talent and intelligence manifesting in the community through the decades, why had the system stagnated, with many schools closed and violent crime increasing? Did the solutions to these problems have to go through so many channels of bureaucracy that nothing was accomplished? Or maybe Laurinburg has become a forgotten place, a swampland with problems some chose not to see, like other small towns across America where factories once shattered the quiet of farm life.

Who can help this beloved town, which contains so much of our rich and proud family history? I thought about Jimmy Carter's Habitat for Humanity, an organization that helps rebuild homes hit by a tornado. Who were the players on the field who could see what was happening here?

I was surprised it had come to this. Growing up in Maryland and attending Howard University in the fast pace of Washington, DC, I was not accustomed to seeing a place with few people and not a chain department store in sight.

To see the story of the Black Malloys a bit more in depth, we traveled to The Malloy/Jordan East Winston Heritage Center in Winston-Salem. Former president George W. Bush sanctioned the building to honor the Malloy and Jordan families, who donated the land to provide a library for the Black community, one of the first at the time. It was named in tribute to two of the Malloy doctors, Henry Darius Malloy and Henry Rembert Malloy, as well as Dr. J. Charles Jordan and their wives. (In Ohio, the William Malloy Center was named for my uncle Braxton.) While we were there, it was great to connect with our cousin Robert Malloy, the former chief of police in Laurinburg, before he passed away, adding to the Malloy legacy.

The library in Winston-Salem features photos as well as stories of the Malloy doctors and family. We took our own photo for our records. Years later, when one of my acting students, Remy Gee, was on a trip looking at colleges, he sent me a photo taken in front of the library after visiting, which allowed me to see that I was following in my grandfather's footsteps by sharing the story of the family with the next generation.

Back in Laurinburg, my mother and I walked down Main Street, once the center of the city filled with major businesses, theaters, hotels, and restaurants. While listening to the local country radio station, we chatted about opening an arts-based school or a restaurant there and brainstormed creative ways to get attention from celebrities, politicians, and influencers.

Seeking a politician to help revive a town can be difficult. Yes, they have the ability to help, but they might not be able to move the needle in terms of land ownership, housing, the wealth gap, or reparations.

In Atlanta, I discovered a new Booker T. Washington, a young real estate developer and investor bearing the same name, who built cost-effective, state-of-the-art, small-scale homes. With these homes he created the first Black-developed microcommunity in the United States, providing more access to home ownership.[1] Perhaps a project like his could help Laurinburg.

Laurinburg's culture shifts as the winds from hurricanes blow. These changes are not just the result of systemic racial blocks but also of economic changes. However, there is still a root that cannot be damaged because it's below the surface. The root is the spirit of the people, a force that cannot be moved, as the elders and their descendants still recall what the town once was.

After enslavement ended, mills provided employment for both

white and Black residents. However dire the conditions, they provided consistent pay for teens and adults. The money from the portion of the mill that the Malloy family owned was fed back into the community, providing low-cost and at times free homes and funding for education efforts. My grandfather often spoke about his role and that of our forefathers in the mill and factory business alongside a partner in one of the largest textile mills in town. The proceeds from the mill provided funds for a few decades after we sold it.

As a child, I would plop onto the brown chair next to where my grandfather was sitting at our house in Maryland. The sofa was his throne, with papers, booklets, cough drops, the broken watches he was repairing, and his phone all surrounding him. I would lean forward with my legs crisscrossed as I tuned in to his story.

When he spoke, I saw the mill and pictured myself taking on my portion of the family business, proudly living the country life our family had always enjoyed. I wanted to upgrade our factory and add a dance studio.

I interrupted his story: "Let's go there and build an upgraded factory I will manage."

Though my dreams at that time were being a doctor and a movie star much like Miss Piggy from *The Muppets Take Manhattan*, I figured that, no matter what, I wouldn't be dependent on the job market. My grandfather always said he would take care of us. I always knew he was happy to hear that I wanted to be a doctor or have a focus on health in some way, following the family tradition. I discovered that he told my mother, when she was a child, "You are going to medical school."

"Laurinburg factory work and farm work were hard," my

grandfather often said, adding, "It was very hard, and everybody had to do their part."

He would tell me about how, as a child, he worked more than he played, and he enjoyed activities such as math games. When he won a competition, he would get only hugs and love pats for it. The family believed that you don't get rewards every time you do good: Doing good is a reward in itself. This practice also keeps down ego, which can tear a family apart.

The textile industry was huge in this little corner of the world, and factories popped up all over North Carolina. This development created an economic surge, a long-lived boom for many North Carolinians, providing great opportunities even for people of color in 1867, when regular employment outside of sharecropping was limited.

The years from 1870 to 1923 were a period of industrial growth in North Carolina. Employees at the mills increased from 300 to 81,000. The South took over in this category, surpassing New England's prominence. Grandpa would exclaim with sound effects, "Wooo ah wooo woo! Can you imagine all of them people? We had a big business!"

White allies, fusionists, and the Black community in Laurinburg followed the ways of the South in protecting and supporting the family. After the 1898 riot in Laurinburg, everyone knew that the riot was not the way of the South, but rather the way of white supremacy.

Laurinburg was very much a "jump in and do it yourself" town without relying on outside sources. The larger your family, the more you could get done, because everyone pitched in to create an empire. I always wanted to have a big family with lots of children after hearing about my grandparents' life. I wanted to live in a town that was a diverse version of the *Andy Griffith* episodes my mom still makes me watch. Having a community that felt like family, working together, seemed incredible.

Many systems were working at once in the Laurinburg community. The predominantly Black area had its own ecosystem following tradition and working to move as one to support the progression of the people while battling outside attacks. The wealthy, predominantly white areas and the lower income areas were vastly different from one another.

Dickson Mill in Laurinburg was known for hiring young white boys. The federal Child Labor Provisions of the Fair Labor Standards Act were not put in place until 1938. Prior to that, it was normal to see young boys working in the mills.

Charles Malloy founded the original Richmond Cotton Mill in 1867, "powered by water wheels. Machinery said to have come from a sunken blockade runner."[2] The blockade runner transported machinery that allowed the textile mill in Scotland County to utilize the advanced techniques used in Europe to create their highly envied fabrics. The needling and tuning and trade secrets of Europe were now in Scotland County for the first time. Now they could emulate the fine fabrics and high fashion of France's elite. Through exports this ignited the fashion industry beyond the Southern states. The mill was leased to Mark Morgan and renamed Morgan Mills in 1872. The Malloys still enjoyed some of the profits after the leasing.

The Springfield Mill helped create a new community in

Scotland County. The work from the mill brought new jobs, which brought new homes to what became Springfield in 1892.

East Laurinburg's Waverly Mill was known for a 1934 strike to protest working conditions that ended in violence, when nine people were wounded by gunshots.

These mills typically gave the surrounding areas a makeover, with churches, businesses, and the community working together. Many in the same household headed to the mill together. Earning an honest wage in the nineteenth and early twentieth centuries often came at the cost of smoke and dust inhalation, poor working conditions, heavy workloads, and dangerous machinery.

By the time my grandfather was a boy, fires, lower costs in other places, and later the Depression caused many of the mills to close or move out of state. With whole communities built around the mills, their closure put hundreds of people out of work and devastated local economies.

Though the cotton mills declined in numbers, new mills and factories took their place in Laurinburg and Scotland County after 1934. Between the Black entrepreneurs and the factory work, the city was buzzing once again. Working conditions improved, and accountability increased with the new labor laws and the protection of unions. Improvements to the machinery caused fewer injuries and deaths, and many employees no longer felt underpaid.

The Southern economy was competitive with that of the North, with all sectors of the country relying on the South's massive cotton production and plethora of products.

I noticed that in conversations with folks in places like New York, people expressed the notion that factory workers and mill workers were mistreated, unfortunate souls. Yet when I talked to folks from the South, I heard that they were upset that the factories and jobs were gone.

Unless you're part of a community that works as a unit and relies on the stability of a company or industry, you cannot understand the gravity of the loss. I wondered, Do we have the mindset to understand the situation if we are not living there or have not spent time there? North Carolina was the mecca of the clothing industry at one time, and we needed the updated factories back in this new post-industrial era.

In 1963, American textiles were the number one commodity, accounting for the sales of 95 percent of all bed linens and clothing in the United States. And North Carolina was leading the way.

The racial composition of American mill workers had shifted by the mid-twentieth century. Per Albert Muzquiz, "Before 1940, only one in ten mill workers was Black—and 80% of those Black positions were as 'mill laborers,' [a] catch-all that mostly meant more work and less pay. But by 1978, one quarter of all mill workers were Black, not just laborers, but proper employees."[3]

The Black community was eager to gain employment in the mills and factories, as it was consistent work. Workers could make their way up the ladder and gain managerial and leadership positions.

The factories were setting the stage for the farm town of Laurinburg to become a factory town. Then NAFTA altered the picture. The 1994 North American Free Trade Agreement did away with the majority of the taxes and tariffs charged for goods at the borders. Business owners in the United States could now trade basically free of charge with Mexico and Canada. This policy helped resolve many trade issues in agriculture, textiles, and automobile manufacturing. Both Republicans and Democrats were involved in the establishment of NAFTA, which was developed under one party and carried out by the other. Many American towns, like Laurinburg, were devastated by the loss of jobs and resources as a result of NAFTA. Years later, NAFTA was re-examined.

Another seismic new policy was enacted under the US-Mexico-Canada Agreement (USMCA), which went into effect on July 1, 2020. NAFTA evolved with readjusted amendments adding a more balanced outcome for the United States. This development allowed more manufacturers and other job-producing industries to be established in the United States.

North Carolina communities would see some small economic improvements; but by the time it trickled down to Laurinburg and other North Carolina towns that had suffered the loss over twenty plus years, the program had a slow impact on joblessness. Some say, regarding factory work, that the new agreement was 90 percent the same as with NAFTA.

These agreements created yet another shift in the character of many cities, including Laurinburg. Members of the global majority, who were the largest population of workers in these factories, lost their jobs. Some workers moved away to find new opportunities, though some saw the agreements as good for the economy. Many key figures, both Democrat and Republican, signed off and championed it.

NAFTA became a polarizing concern for many officials. Some people were opposed to the agreement and feared it would devastate communities that relied on the factories. Others felt NAFTA would boost towns with a new type of business when the factories closed. Before NAFTA, when the factories became dominant, there were health and safety concerns, but workers found that factory jobs were less stressful than farming and made possible a better-quality home life.

In their heyday, North Carolina factories produced national consumer items such as cotton textiles—blankets, sheets, clothing, fabric—and metal products in addition to the fruits and vegetables from year-round farming.

In June 2023, my mother and I talked with Cousin Wilbur Malloy about NAFTA and Laurinburg. Wilbur still owns property there and is a retired US Army lieutenant colonel who helped make vital medical advancements during Desert Storm in Saudi Arabia.

"In the early 1960s, say, Cannon, one of the largest manufacturers of towels, had their plants in Scotland County," Wilbur told us. "Freight shoes for trains were made in Scotland County, and so was automobile glass manufactured for cars. The list goes on and on. All these factories were in the vicinity of what used to be the Laurinburg-Maxton Air Base. Today they've all moved away to places where it's easy to find cheap labor. . . . Laurinburg has been affected by that tremendously."

North Carolina legislators tried to create policies for change. When everyone went to work at the factories, they grew accustomed to a lifestyle that included cars and new homes. But the odds were against having these economic opportunities over the long haul.

The closing of the factories in Scotland County would have a domino effect. The lack of employment also led to an increase in crime. Poverty breeds crime when people need to survive but have few opportunities to do so.

How do we recover and restore the ashes of our people, our homes, and our communities that have been taken and hidden from us? Laurinburg prospered at its height when the Black and white communities came together to focus on farms, education, and representation from the Black community. There is also a large Native American community in Scotland County with an extensive history. Will the next generation of Scotland County thinkers have access to the stories of the town?

As my mother and I rode through the community where our family once lived, the secret haven that existed jumped out at us at every turn. The misty warm weather, the peaceful chirping of the birds, the green of the farms, and the serenity of the homes brought solace. Because of the town's isolation from the noise and lights of the big cities, Laurinburg seemed like an ideal family town at half the cost of city living.

As the sun changed places with the moon, the long, dark roads of the country at night were picturesque. Branches from the hovering trees hit the car, and the leaves caught the glow from the headlights. Every other road led to a longer one that would return us to a road we had just gotten off: It seemed as if we couldn't leave the area. We passed by our properties several times before we found the way out. The hardships Laurinburg has faced, from war to extreme weather to racism, are visible as you ride through the town or look it up online. As we passed by the same streets yet again, I wondered, will Laurinburg ever be what it once was?

I've joined my mother in her research often in the past ten years, speaking with librarians, church officials, community members, and others. Each time she shared some of the unique stories she had gathered, she made others happy. The pride in Laurinburg was still there.

Many of the people we spoke with said they wanted to see the town revived, including the pastors at Laurel Hill Church, the staff at Laurinburg Library, Wilbur Malloy, and Frank "Bishop" McDuffie. Families have left their homes and land standing empty as they have found more opportunities elsewhere. It can be a challenge to connect the changemakers to those who have not yet burned out from the constant struggle, but it's not a greater challenge than the ones that William and other Laurinburg residents faced years earlier.

One step in the right direction would be lifting the extensive taxes on land to allow the families to return and retrieve their property, if still available. Repurposing areas for affordable, diverse communities of all incomes could help fill empty homes. Well-paying jobs could narrow the wealth gap and improve living conditions for many, as would tax incentives encouraging large conglomerates to come to Laurinburg and Scotland County.

Using donations to hire a community planner could help gather support for the cause and reach millions of social media users. Many folks are in search of a little town away from the big city hustle and bustle, particularly one with nice weather.

As we worked on this book, alternating writing and researching together, my mother and I came across an exciting development. On November 2, 2023, North Carolina governor Roy Cooper sanctioned a $9.7 million grant to create affordable homes in Laurinburg. The I. Ellis Johnson Multifamily Housing facility is set to provide high-quality homes for residents. The Southeastern Community Action Partnership (SCAP), North Carolina Housing Finance Agency, F. Diane Honeycutt Center at Richmond Community College, early learning programs, and the first statewide collaboration with public schools, community colleges, and private universities will also benefit from the grant funds. The Laurinburg city manager says that millions of dollars will be put into revitalizing downtown and Main Street.[4] Bishop McDuffie at Laurinburg Institute once suggested repurposing the town's vacant buildings for artists' studios, theaters for actors, and sports arenas.

Today the local government pushes to make changes, such as naming areas downtown where live concerts echo throughout the town after the McDuffie family. Black journalists pen pieces about the history of the town for *The Laurinburg Exchange*. There are online videos celebrating the lovely Christmas decorations set up on Main Street and downtown. And in 2023, a group of chain restaurants came to town, including Popeyes on Main Street.

Films such as *Rebound: The Legend of Earl "The Goat" Manigault*, starring Don Cheadle and directed by Eriq La Salle, have highlighted the town and its historical Black community. Restoration of the town and the Institute is ongoing with the help of many people.

As the town works to restore its economy, it is also time to restore the history that may not be obvious but that can be found in the soil, in the homes, and in the stories passed down through families. This full restoration is the foundation on which we can rebuild. I am the fourth-generation child of the Malloy family, yet I feel I knew my grandfather William and Laurinburg through family stories and my mother's research.

I've come to recognize the importance of listening attentively to every elder. Each story, no matter how old, offers me a new part of my own story. By listening, I learned about three of the first doctors in Laurinburg and Winston-Salem: William Murphy, William Braxton, and my father's first cousin Henry Rembert Malloy, who was the first Black person in the South to have a practice focused on surgery.

My grandparents were proud of their accomplishments and would not stand being discriminated against. Their case against the Wilson Line resulted in new policies in Washington, DC, Virginia, and Maryland, and was recently cited on historical websites for Baltimore, Maryland.

Taking this journey with my mother allowed me to dive deeper into the events that informed her life and the story of the town that shaped my ancestors.

Acknowledgments

One year, my daughter and I were asked by the late Broadway star James Stovall and Broadway producer Voza Rivers to perform at the American Museum of Natural History for Kwanzaa. Throughout the day, over thirty thousand people attended this joy-filled celebration. Before it could start, the audience was asked to name ancestors who impacted their life; as the names were spoken aloud in honor, water was poured into a vase in a symbolic offering to them.

After the libation, the host asked the elders present for permission to proceed with the show. We could not move forward without honoring and showing gratitude to them and to the ancestors.

This process reminded me of the rituals my parents performed at their events and parties, honoring the past and the present. At the end of every party, my father would say, loud and clear, "Thank you all for coming. Now come watch yourself on television." Everyone would gather on the second floor of 804 Hyde Road in Silver Spring, Maryland, and stand around the television, waiting to see themselves. My father called out their names as their faces passed across the screen. Smiles and jolts of laughter punctuated each

ACKNOWLEDGMENTS

moment. This was my parents' way of honoring those who made the community what it was.

To close this book, we would like to offer gratitude and a written libation to the ancestors, elders, and everyone else who touched this work and/or supported our journey in honoring and celebrating family, culture, and community.

The process of moving ten years of research into a narrative that shines a light on many aspects of my family and their community would have been a daunting task without Patricia Mulcahy's expertise and assistance. Thank you for your tireless support, lengthy phone calls, and editing, and for being a guiding force in writing our first book.

To our editor, Patrik Bass, and everyone at Amistad: This book is precious to us, bringing out the stories of our family and many other families as well as those of the town they cherished. We are so grateful to be starting our journey as authors with you. Patrik, your commitment to making sure this story was told with honor and care has meant the world to us.

We started this journey three years ago with Karen Murgolo of Aevitas Creative Management. Thank you for believing in our promise as authors and seeing the full potential and value of these stories. We look forward to continuing to share important stories with your guidance and support.

Cousin Wilbur Malloy sat for hours of phone calls over the past decade as we asked questions and shared research and information about the history of the Malloy family and Laurinburg. Thank you for sharing your stories of growing up in Laurinburg, for supporting our efforts to document the family, and for holding on to the land, keeping it in the Malloy name. My father was always so happy to see you when you stopped by our house in Maryland. He was instantly transported back to Laurinburg at the sight of your smile.

ACKNOWLEDGMENTS

Over the past ten years, Frank "Bishop" McDuffie has become family. From our early talks about teaching at Laurinburg Institute to sharing stories of our families' efforts to restore and preserve the history of the town, our talks with Bishop were always so fruitful. Thank you! The best is yet to come.

The on-point advice and wisdom of Earl Smith about the potential of these stories and the importance of education in the Black community kept us moving forward. Thank you.

My mother's last sister, Aunt Myrtle Butler, listened with open ears as we talked through each new piece of history we learned and was quick to tell us if we had our facts wrong. Thank you for always being present with advice and being open and willing to share.

Meghan Thomas, thank you for lending us your talents as we first gathered this story and for your willingness to support our efforts. We look forward to working with you in the future and remain fans of your writing.

Thank you to the late Lawrence and Loncie Malloy, the late Dorothy Robinson, the late Fairley Mae McCoy, and the late Grace Thomas for the stories and being driving forces in our lives, and supporting us on many levels. We have memories to cherish forever. Ase'.

Larry "Leon" Malloy, thank you for providing family stories and thoughts and the needed institutional knowledge of the family.

To our family in Cleveland and Washington, DC, Tracy Thomas, the Norwoods, the Milgates, the Carters, the Butlers, the Warrens, the Kinds, Daryl Solomon, Karen Williams and family, and the Whitfields, thank you for the phone calls, care, and support.

To the late Bernadine Thomas for being one of our biggest cheerleaders: You couldn't wait for this book after sharing stories for years. Mobetta and Nay Nay love you always.

ACKNOWLEDGMENTS

Charisse Williams, we are grateful for your continued encouragement in our arts journey, the many days of traveling to NYC, and your always celebrating the work we do.

Doretha Ann Noble-Brown and family, thank you for being there whenever needed, giving words of inspiration and care as well as support.

Thank you to Nae Malloy, for the needed conversations and sharing your history with us, and to all other family members who have supported our efforts, we are grateful.

To our other Laurinburg connections and dear family friends, Nathaniel and Mary McLaurin and Dan and Betty McLaurin, thank you for sharing stories with us and being lifelong friends of the family.

Over the years we have spoken on the phone with and visited libraries, churches, and museums, working with incredible staff, researchers, and librarians who answered the phone, sent emails, provided photos, and returned calls with needed information and welcoming conversations. Thank you to the Malloy/Jordan East Winston Heritage Center in Winton Salem, North Carolina; Chapel Hill Public Library; Scotland County Memorial Library; the Church of Jesus Christ of Latter-Day Saints Library in Kensington, Maryland; the Scottish Heritage Center in Laurinburg; the University of Strathclyde; Johnson C. Smith University for giving us permission to use the photo of Uncle Emmett; the Presbyterian Historical Society, Philadelphia, PA, that provided the photo of our family at the Barber-Scotia Summer Learning Program; the Massillon Museum for the photo of Uncle Braxton (William Braxton); and the Smithsonian National Museum of African American History and Culture (Gift of James M. Baxter) for the photo of McNeely's Blacksmith in Laurinburg, North Carolina.

Dr. Soyica Colbert provided a needed note on the importance of stories like these being told from a multigenerational perspective.

ACKNOWLEDGMENTS

She and Dr. Mary Helen Washington advised on ways to make it happen. We are grateful to have such wise and powerful writers in our lives. Thank you!

Thank you, Deb Moss, for shining a light on the alma mater you share with our family, Johnson C. Smith University.

Thank you to Howard University for being a source of higher education for our family for generations, instilling pride and rigor in our efforts as only an HBCU can. Thank you to the Howard University professors who stayed connected beyond class, guiding our writing and research and providing support and encouragement to write these stories and celebrate family: the late Dr. Ralph Gomes, Dr. Ara Thomas-Brown, Professor LaVerne Reed, Dr. Lorraine Henry, Fred Irby III, Kim Bey, Dr. Linda Heywood, Mike Malone, Joe Selmon, and many more. We consider you family.

To our friends who helped us explore ways to share the stories far and wide while expanding our knowledge of the entertainment industry, Archie Gips and Unrealistic Ideas and Erika Alexander and Color Farm Media, thank you for connecting with the family story and letting us know the possibilities. We appreciate you.

To our friends who went above and beyond, listened and encouraged and offered support and care, whether by engaging in long phone calls, sharing stories, reading drafts, or providing a place of respite: Andrea Urrutia, Vikki Mason, Colette Magwood, Nicole Brewer, Charles Leath, Bernie Davallier, L'Tanya Marie Rivas for the lovely websites, Carol S. Braswell, Karen Daniels, Rita Wilson, Dat Ngo, Ayanda Pyramid, Genia Lear Morgan, Mary Slimp, Nicole Mebane, Nikaury Rodriguez, Colleen Longshaw Jackson, Kristra Forney, Reigna Celeste, Dr. Tyrone Stanley, Claybourne Chavers, Esq., Dr. Clifton Coates, Diezel Braxton-Lewis, Frenchie Davis, Tammy and Abena Green, and the late Dr. Cissy Houston, we thank you!

ACKNOWLEDGMENTS

Ashley, Wolfgang, and Reign, we are so grateful to have you in our lives. What a journey together over the years. Ashley, thank you for taking us in and supporting our efforts in every way you could. We are grateful and appreciate you on many levels.

Valerie Knapp, thank you for joining this journey years ago as we navigated the process and for being a sounding board; your endless support and friendship are greatly appreciated. Smita P. Patel, RPh, thank you for your care. Joannie Danielides, Charlotte Moore, Judy Tate, Chris Jennings, and Frankie Bethea, we thank you.

In our research, we discovered that the families of two of our oldest friends, Kristen Jackson and Phyllis Williams, Esq., were connected to our family in Laurinburg—a major highlight! When my father heard the name Jackson and discovered it was the same family that frequented his home in Laurinburg, his smile lit up the house. Thank you for listening, always being supportive, and sharing your knowledge with us.

Thank you to lifelong family friends Cindy and Bob Gerstl, for the living room chats. We loved learning more about your family, journey, and experience from across the street. Thank you to the rest of the Kemp Mill family, the late Jeanne Adams Daniels, the Cahills, Lucy Hayes, the late Shirley Catalan, the late Naomi Waddleton, the late Carrie Hughley, Earnest Leach Jr., the late Myron, Abbadean Robertson, and many more.

To Erin Shultz, thank you for connecting us with Arianna Huffington and for your efforts.

Dr. Phyllis Lee Viccellio, thank you for your guidance navigating the world of writing over the past twenty-seven years and for being a continual support in our efforts and journey as artists.

Shakespeare Theatre Company family, Tappers with Attitude and Knock on Wood, and Harvard University Center for Hellenic

ACKNOWLEDGMENTS

Studies, we are grateful for you. Tim Fowler, thank you for giving LeeAnét a book that helped to pave this path.

We thank the faith families that supported our efforts and provided spaces for us over the years: Northwood Presbyterian Church, Greater Washington Deliverance Temple, and Union Temple Baptist Church.

And to everyone who has touched our lives, listened to the stories, and exchanged support, we appreciate you.

Notes

Introduction

1. Richard Rothstein, *The Color of Law: A Forgotten History of How Our Government Segregated America* (Liveright, 2017), 177.

2. Jillian Diamond, "'Not in My Neighborhood': A Montgomery County Project Maps the Story of Antisemitic, Racist Housing Laws," *Washington Jewish Week*, June 22, 2023, https://www.washingtonjewishweek.com/not-in-my-neighborhood-a-montgomery-county-project-maps-the-story-of-antisemitic-racist-housing-laws/.

3. Eugene L. Meyer, "A Shameful Past: A Look at Montgomery County's History of Racism," Moco60.Media, March 29, 2021, https://moco360.media/2021/03/29/a-shameful-past/.

4. Lawrence Malloy Sr., "Seeds of Love" and "Postmaster" (self-published, years unknown).

5. Loncie L. Malloy, "Black Jobless Rate," *Jet*, May 8, 1975, 4.

6. W. E. B. Du Bois, *The Autobiography of W. E. B. Du Bois: A Soliloquy on Viewing My Life from the Last Decade of Its First Century*, 10th ed. (International Publishers, 1968), 95.

7. Louis B. Bryan, "Brief History of Fred R. Moore, Editor New York Age," manuscript dated November 6, 1936, Schomburg Center for Research in Black Culture, Manuscripts, Archives and Rare Books Division, New York Public Library Digital Collections, accessed May 1, 2024, https://

NOTES

digitalcollections.nypl.org/items/3b052450-79bd-0133-bb56-00505686d14e.

8. "Tim Wise Part 3 - The History of Whiteness," San Jose City College, June 8, 2020, video, https://www.youtube.com/watch?v=dfJAp7NwgVA.

9. Linda Tarrant-Reid, *Discovering Black America: From the Age of Exploration to the Twenty-First Century* (Abrams, 2012), 27.

1. Africans, Scots, and Americans

1. Nettie McCormick Henley, *The Home Place* (Vantage Press, 1955), 64.

2. "The Gaelic Speaking Slaves of 18th Century America," *The Scotsman*, March 5, 2018, https://www.scotsman.com/arts-and-culture/the-gaelic-speaking-slaves-of-18th-century-america-559162.

3. Henley, *The Home Place*, 2.

4. James Roderick Macdonald, "Cultural Retention and Adaptation Among Highland Scots of Carolina," PhD thesis, University of Edinburgh, September 1992; "Gabriel Johnston: Royal Governor of North Carolina Province, 1734 to 1752," Carolana, https://www.carolana.com/NC/Royal_Colony/gjohnson.html.

5. "Passenger Vessels Act 1803," Lex Justis, accessed April 12, 2013, https://vlex.co.uk/vid/passenger-vessels-act-1803-808496565.

6. Macdonald, "Cultural Retention and Adaptation."

7. Macdonald, "Cultural Retention and Adaptation."

8. U. R. Taylor and Lindsey Brush, "Black History Month - Week 2," University of Connecticut, published February 9, 2023, https://publications.extension.uconn.edu/2023/02/09/black-history-month-week-2/.

9. Kinshasha Holman Conwill, ed., *We Return Fighting: World War I and the Shaping of Modern Black Identity* (Soho Press, 2019), 52–53.

10. "Murdoch Morrison Gun Factory," forum discussion, Civil War Talk, January 25, 2016, https://civilwartalk.com/threads/murdoch-morrison-gun-factory.121024/.

11. Henry L. Gates Jr. and Kwame Anthony Appiah, eds., *Africana: The Encyclopedia of the African and African American Experience*, 5 vols. (Basic Civitas Books, 1999), 1728–34.

12. Andrew D. Weinberger, "A Reappraisal of the Constitutionality of Miscegenation Statutes," *Journal of Negro Education* 26, no. 4 (1957): 435–46.

13. "A Reappraisal of the Constitutionality of Miscegenation Statutes," APPSTATE 125, Appalachian State University, https://dsi.appstate.edu/projects/lumbee/wein001.

14. "The Civil War: The Senate's Story," United States Senate, The Secretary of the Senate, https://www.senate.gov/artandhistory/history/common/generic/Civil_War_AdmissionReadmission.htm.

2. 1865

1. Hattie E. Buell, "A Child of the King," *Northern Christian Advocate*, 1877.

2. Patricia B. Whitfield, "African Americans and the Reluctance to Seek Treatment," American Counseling Association, September 1, 2021, https://www.counseling.org/publications/counseling-today-magazine/article-archive/article/legacy/african-americans-and-the-reluctance-to-seek-treatment.

3. "G. Stanley Hall American Psychologist," Britannica, January 28, 2028, https://www.britannica.com/science/evolutionary-psychology/Controversy.

4. Hope M. Hill, "Exposure to Community Violence and Social Support as Predictors of Anxiety and Social and Emotional Behavior Among African American Children," *Journal of Child and Family Studies* 5 (1996): 399–414.

5. H. L. Brumberg, D. Dozor, and S. G. Golombek, "History of the Birth Certificate: From Inception to the Future of Electronic Data," *Journal of Perinatology* 32, no. 6 (February 2012): 407–11.

6. John Shelton Reed and Dale Volberg Reed, *1001 Things Everyone Should Know About the South* (Doubleday, 2007), 6.

NOTES

7. W. E. B. Du Bois, *Black Reconstruction in America: An Essay Toward a History of the Part Which Black Folk Played in the Attempt to Reconstruct Democracy in America, 1860–1880*, 3rd ed. (Free Press, 1998).

8. "African Americans in the Civil War," National Park Service, accessed February 25, 2025, https://www.nps.gov/chyo/learn/historyculture/african-americans-in-the-civil-war.htm.

9. Shirley J. Yee, *Black Women Abolitionists: Study in Activism, 1828–1860* (Univ. of Tennessee Press, 1992), 6.

10. David S. Reynolds, *John Brown, Abolitionist: The Man Who Killed Slavery, Sparked the Civil War, and Seeded Civil Rights* (Vintage, 2006).

11. Frederick Douglass, quoted in Henry L. Gates Jr., *Stony the Road: Reconstruction, White Supremacy, and the Rise of Jim Crow* (Penguin Press, 2019), 11.

12. John Hope Franklin and Alfred A. Moss Jr., *From Slavery to Freedom: A History of African Americans*, 8th ed. (Alfred A. Knopf, 2002).

13. Richard Edwards, "African American Homesteaders in the Great Plains," National Park Service, US Department of the Interior, https://www.nps.gov/articles/african-american-homesteaders-in-the-great-plains.htm.

14. Mark Morgan and Laurel Hill, "Personal Capitalism," *International Social Science Review* 67, no. 2 (1992): 69.

15. Leah Douglass, "African Americans Have Lost Untold Acres of Land Over the Last Century," *The Nation*, July 17, 2017, https://www.thenation.com/article/archive/african-americans-have-lost-acres/.

16. "A Brief History of Black Land Ownership in the U.S.," Fair Farms Now, March 25, 2021, https://fairfarmsnow.org/black-land-ownership-in-the-maryland-farming-community/.

17. Eric Foner, "Reconstruction," Britannica, February 15, 2025, https://www.britannica.com/event/American-Civil-War.

18. "The Civil War in America: John S. Rock," Library of Congress, accessed February 25, 2025, https://www.loc.gov/exhibits/civil-war-in-america/biographies/john-s-rock.html.

19. "Abraham Lincoln: Speech at New Haven," The History Place, accessed August 19, 2024, www.historyplace.com/lincoln/haven.htm.

NOTES

20. *Black Stage: Classical Canon*, WHUT TV, February 26, 2025, video, 19 min., 6 sec., https://www.youtube.com/watch?v=EA2JS6kAx-oY&t=78s.

21. Michael Les Benedict, "Southern Democrats in the Crisis of 1876–1877: A Reconsideration of Reunion and Reaction," *Journal of Southern History* 46 (1980): 489–524.

22. Alex Sandifer and Betty Dishong Renfer, "Schools for Freed Peoples," *Tar Heel Junior Historian* 37, no. 1 (Fall 1997), https://www.ncpedia.org/education/freed-peoples.

23. Langston Hughes, *Montage of a Dream Deferred* (Henry Holt and Company, 1951), 71.

3. Grandfather William

1. W. E. B. Du Bois, *Black Reconstruction in America: An Essay Toward a History of the Part Which Black Folk Played in the Attempt to Reconstruct Democracy in America, 1860–1880*, 3rd ed. (Free Press, 1998), 3.

2. Paul Heinegg, *Free African Americans of North Carolina, Virginia, and South Carolina from the Colonial Period to About 1820* (Clearfield, 2001).

3. Nettie McCormick Henley, *The Home Place* (Vantage Press, 1955), 14–16.

4. Mary L. Coleman, "Chapel Hill Church Laurinburg, NC," *Africo-American Presbyterian* (Wilmington), October 11, 1934.

5. Christine Andreae, "Slave Medicine," Monticello, accessed February 25, 2025, https://www.monticello.org/sites/library/exhibits/lucymarks/medical/slavemedicine.html.

6. Henley, *The Home Place*, 2.

7. Frank T. Wilson, "Living Witnesses: Black Presbyterians in Ministry, III," *Journal of Presbyterian History* 55, no. 2 (1977): 210.

4. People and Places

1. "The Road to Secession," North Carolina Historic Sites, accessed February 19, 2025, https://historicsites.nc.gov/resources/north-carolina-civil-war/road-secession.

NOTES

2. Kamala Harris (@KamalaHarris), "Our unity is our strength, and our diversity is our power. We reject the myth of 'us' vs. 'them,'" Twitter, July 21, 2016, https://x.com/KamalaHarris/status/756219715832250368.

3. Christine B. Hickman, "The Devil and the One Drop Rule: Racial Categories, African Americans, and the U.S. Census," *Michigan Law Review* 95 (1997): 1161–265.

4. Mary Bellis, "How the Telephone Was Invented," ThoughtCo., September 20, 2024, https://www.thoughtco.com/history-of-the-telephone-alexander-graham-bell-1991380.

5. "About Us," *Laurinburg Exchange*, https://www.laurinburgexchange.com/about-us.

6. *The Laurinburg Post*, December 21, 1895, edition 1, https://newspapers.digitalnc.org/lccn/sn91068174/1895-12-21/ed-1/seq-1/#pageinformation.

7. "Finding News Stories: Black Newspapers in North Carolina," University Libraries, University of North Carolina, https://guides.lib.unc.edu/news-Stories/AfAm-NC.

8. Maxcy L. John, "Historical Sketch of Laurinburg," *Laurinburg Exchange*, June 29, 1916: 2.

9. L. J. Alonge, "Writing Past the White Gaze as a Black Author," *Code Switch*, National Public Radio, March 4, 2017, https://www.npr.org/sections/codeswitch/2017/03/04/515790514/writing-past-the-white-gaze-as-a-black-author.

10. "N F McEachin," Find a Grave, https://www.findagrave.com/memorial/143570175/n-f-mceachin.

5. A Backyard War

1. H. Leon Prather Sr., "The Red Shirt Movement in North Carolina 1898–1900," *Journal of Negro History* 62, no. 2 (1977): 174, https://www.jstor.org/stable/2717177?read-now=1&seq=1#page_scan_tab_contents.

2. Brian Kilmeade, *Teddy and Booker T.: How Two American Icons Blazed a Path for Racial Equality* (Sentinel, 2023), 181.

3. Kilmeade, *Teddy and Booker T.*, 185.

NOTES

4. Gael Graham, "'The Lexington of White Supremacy': School and Local Politics in Late-Nineteenth-Century Laurinburg, North Carolina," *North Carolina Historical Review* 89, no. 1 (2012): 27–58, http://www.jstor.org/stable/23523943.

5. Graham, "'The Lexington of White Supremacy.'"

6. Nettie McCormick Henley, *The Home Place* (Vantage Press, 1955), 16.

7. Henley, *The Home Place*, 17.

8. Henley, *The Home Place*, 16.

9. Graham, "'The Lexington of White Supremacy.'"

10. "White Men Show Determination to Rid Themselves of Negro Rule," *Morning Star* (Wilmington), November 2, 1898, https://newspapers.digitalnc.org/lccn/sn84026537/1898-11-02/ed-1/seq-1/.

11. "White Men Show Determination to Rid Themselves of Negro Rule."

12. Candace Dantes, "7 Scarring Facts, Figures About America's Black Belt Region People," Black Farmers' Network, January 13, 2021, https://blackfarmersnetwork.com/7-scarring-facts-figures-about-americas-black-belt-region/.

13. Prather, "The Red Shirt Movement in North Carolina."

14. "White Men Show Determination to Rid Themselves of Negro Rule."

15. "A Day of Blood at Wilmington," *News and Observer* (Raleigh), November 11, 1898, https://newspapers.digitalnc.org/lccn/sn85042104/1898-11-11/ed-1/seq-1/.

16. "White Men Show Determination to Rid Themselves of Negro Rule."

17. Graham, "'The Lexington of White Supremacy.'"

18. Graham, "'The Lexington of White Supremacy.'"

19. Graham, "'The Lexington of White Supremacy.'"

6. Post-Insurrection

1. Brian Kilmeade, *Teddy and Booker T.: How Two American Icons Blazed a Path for Racial Equality* (Sentinel, 2023), 185–86.

NOTES

2. Kilmeade, *Teddy and Booker T.*, 186.

3. "A Red Record," accessed April 22, 2025, https://lynching.web.unc.edu/.

4. Nettie McCormick Henley, *The Home Place* (Vantage Press, 1955), 58.

5. Gael Graham, "'The Lexington of White Supremacy': School and Local Politics in Late-Nineteenth-Century Laurinburg, North Carolina," *North Carolina Historical Review* 89, no. 1 (2012): 27–58.

6. Graham, "'The Lexington of White Supremacy.'"

7. Booker T. Washington, *Up from Slavery* (Doubleday Page & Company, 1907).

8. Graham, "'The Lexington of White Supremacy.'"

9. Patrick Minges, "Beneath the Underdog: Race, Religion, and the Trail of Tears," U.S. Data Repository, updated 1998, https://www.us-data.org/us/minges/underdog.html.

10. Frederick Douglass, "The Hutchinson Family—Hunkerism," *North Star* (Rochester), October 27, 1848.

11. "North Carolina Railroads: Laurinburg and Southern Railroad," NC Home, accessed February 21, 2025, https://www.carolana.com/NC/Transportation/railroads/nc_rrs_laurinburg_southern.html.

12. Dylan C. Penningroth, *Before the Movement: The Hidden History of Black Civil Rights* (Liveright, 2023), 322.

13. "Africa, Portugal," South African History Online, September 11, 2011, https://www.sahistory.org.za/article/africa-portugal.

14. F. James Davis, *Who Is Black? One Nation's Definition*, 20th ed. (Pennsylvania State Univ. Press, 1991).

7. Another New Beginning

1. Booker T. Washington, "The Atlanta Exposition Address Part 2," National Park Service, February 26, 2015, https://www.nps.gov/bowa/learn/historyculture/atlanta2-1.htm.

2. Shomari Wills, *Black Fortunes: The Story of the First Six African Americans Who Escaped Slavery and Became Millionaires* (Amistad, 2018), 191.

NOTES

3. Rebekah Dobrasko, "The Rosenwald Schools: Progressive Era Philanthropy in the Segregated South," Teaching with Historic Places lesson plan, National Park Service, June 2015, https://www.nps.gov/articles/the-rosenwald-schools-progressive-era-philanthropy-in-the-segregated-south-teaching-with-historic-places.htm.

4. Jael Pembrick, "History Hidden in Plain Sight," *Laurinburg Exchange*, February 7, 2019, https://www.laurinburgexchange.com/news/22483/history-hidden-in-plain-sight.

5. Philip A. Mackowiak, "Booker T. Washington and the Secret of Hypertension in African Americans," *American Journal of the Medical Sciences* 352, no. 4 (2016): 416–19.

6. W. H. Weatherspoon, "Auction Sale of Desirable City Property," *Laurinburg Exchange*, November 14, 1918, https://newspapers.digitalnc.org/lccn/sn91068179/1918-11-14/ed-1/seq-2.pdf.

7. "'Aunt Becky' Writes of Crops and Travels," *Laurinburg Exchange*, July 4, 1918, https://newspapers.digitalnc.org/lccn/sn91068179/1918-07-04/ed-1/seq-1/.

8. "A Sampling of Jim Crow Laws," NCpedia, accessed March 5, 2025, https://www.ncpedia.org/anchor/sampling-jim-crow-laws.

9. Peter Bean, "Fellow Examines Life in North Carolina Under Jim Crow," Wilson Center, June 3, 2004, https://www.wilsoncenter.org/article/fellow-examines-life-north-carolina-under-jim-crow.

10. "Founding of the NAACP," History, March 29, 2023, https://www.history.com/topics/black-history/naacp.

11. Donna R. Braden, "Black Entrepreneurs During the Jim Crow Era," The Henry Ford, February 21, 2018, https://www.thehenryford.org/explore/blog/black-entrepreneurs-during-the-jim-crow-era/.

12. Linda Tarrant-Reid, *Discovering Black America: From the Age of Exploration to the Twenty-First Century* (Abrams, 2012), 126.

8. Southern Tea

1. Maya Prabhu and Jessica Gergen, "History's Seven Deadliest Plagues," Gavi, November 15, 2021, https://www.gavi.org/vaccineswork/historys-seven-deadliest-plagues.

NOTES

2. "Malloy, William B," Black Soldiers Mattered, https://www.blacksoldiersmattered.com/soldier?id=WW-I-Card_World-War-I-Service-Card-4-c_02967.tif.

3. "Malloy, William B."

4. "Barber-Scotia Junior College," (advertisement), *Africo-American Presbyterian* (Wilmington), April 6, 1933, https://newspapers.digitalnc.org/lccn/sn84025826/1933-04-06/ed-1/seq-3/.

5. Santiago Delboy, "How Trauma Affects Our Sense of Time," Fermata Psychotherapy, https://www.fermatapsychotherapy.com/blog/2023/4/14/how-trauma-affects-our-sense-of-time.

6. JJ Melton, "'The Local Legend of Spaghetti,'" *Laurinburg Exchange*, September 18, 2020, https://www.laurinburgexchange.com/news/41427/the-local-legend-of-spaghetti.

7. Herbert K. Fox, "Things You Want to Know About Scotland County," *Laurinburg Exchange*, May 15, 1924, 41.

8. "Africo-American Presbyterian (Wilmington, N.C.) 1879–1938," Library of Congress, https://www.loc.gov/item/sn84025826/.

9. George R. Marsh, "The Eastern District Sunday School of Yadkin Presbytery," *Africo-American Presbyterian*, October 1, 1925.

10. George R. Marsh, "In and Out and Round and About in Yadkin Presbytery," *Africo-American Presbyterian*, September 23, 1926, 38.

11. "Annie Malloy" (obituary), *New York Age*, August 18, 1928, 7.

9. Coming of Age

1. Howard E. Covington Jr. and Marion A. Ellis, *Terry Sanford: Politics, Progress, and Outrageous Ambitions* (Duke Univ. Press, 1999), 15.

2. Covington and Ellis, *Terry Sanford*, 16.

3. "Laurinburg, NC," *New York Age*, June 15, 1929, 7.

4. Marilyn Wright, "Laurinburg Normal and Industrial Institute," North Carolina Encyclopedia, 2006, https://www.ncpedia.org/laurinburg-normal-and-industrial-in.

5. Dizzy Gillespie with Al Fraser, *To Be, or Not . . . to Bop* (Univ. of Minnesota Press, 2009), 35.
6. Alyn Shipton, *Groovin' High: The Life of Dizzy Gillespie* (Oxford Univ. Press, 2001), 13.
7. Phoebe Ann Pollitt, *African American Hospitals in North Carolina: 39 Institutional Histories, 1880–1967* (McFarland Incorporated, 2017), 140.
8. Wilbur Malloy, personal communication with authors, June 10, 2023.
9. "Other State News," *New York Age*, July 30, 1932, 8.
10. "Laurinburg, NC," *New York Age*, October 8, 1932, 10.
11. "Laurinburg, NC" (obituary), *New York Age*, December 26, 1931, 8.
12. Covington and Ellis, *Terry Sanford*, 21.
13. Mary L. Coleman, "Chapel Hill Church Laurinburg, NC," *Africo-American Presbyterian* (Wilmington), October 11, 1934, https://newspapers.digitalnc.org/lccn/sn84025826/1934-10-11/ed-1/seq-3/.
14. "Bowers Chapel Church Laurinburg, NC," *Africo-American Presbyterian* (Wilmington), June 13, 1935, 4.
15. "Walter P. Evans Passes at Laurinburg," *Africo-American Presbyterian* (Wilmington), March 13, 1937, 2.
16. Tyler Bamford, "African Americans Fought for Freedom at Home and Abroad During World War II," National WWII Museum, February 1, 2020, https://www.nationalww2museum.org/war/articles/african-americans-fought-freedom-home-and-abroad-during-world-war-ii.

10. Country to Town

1. Alexis Clark, "Returning from War, Returning to Racism," *New York Times*, July 30, 2020, www.nytimes.com/2020/07/30/magazine/black-soldiers-wwii-racism.html.
2. Clark, "Returning from War."
3. Clark, "Returning from War."

NOTES

4. Erin Blakemore, "How the GI Bill's Promise Was Denied to a Million Black WWII Veterans," History, June 21, 2023, https://www.history.com/news/gi-bill-black-wwii-veterans-benefits.

5. "Laurinburg-Maxton Army Air Base (K-63) K-63," North Carolina Department of Natural and Cultural Resources, January 11, 2024, https://www.dncr.nc.gov/blog/2024/01/11/laurinburg-maxton-army-air-base-k-63.

6. "About Africo-American Presbyterian (Wilmington, N.C.) 1879–1938," Library of Congress, https://www.loc.gov/item/sn84025826/.

7. "Press Photo Tornado Damage in Laurinburg, N.C.," August 29, 1940, Historic Images, https://historicimages.com/products/rsd57445.

8. "Redlining," Federal Reserve History, June 2, 2023, https://www.federalreservehistory.org/essays/redlining.

9. "Boat Company Ordered to End Lily-White Policy by ICC," *Afro-American*, November 24, 1951, 22, https://news.google.com/newspapers?id=ltQmAAAAIBAJ&sjid=kgIGAAAAIBAJ&pg=1269%2C2421874.

10. "Boat Company Ordered to End Lily-White Policy by ICC."

11. "Boat Company Ordered to End Lily-White Policy by ICC."

12. Interstate Commerce Commission Reports, No.30769, November 2, 1951, 362.

11. Going Back to Move Forward

1. J. L. Hochschild and B. M. Powell, "Racial Reorganization and the United States Census 1850–1930: Mulattoes, Half-Breeds, Mixed Parentage, Hindoos, and the Mexican Race," *Studies in American Political Development* 22, no. 1 (2008): 59.

2. Cheris Hodges, "A Strong Legacy," *Laurinburg Exchange*, December 17, 2015, https://www.laurinburgexchange.com/news/55611/a-strong-legacy.

3. US Department of Commerce, "Current Population Reports," August 10, 1966, Census.gov, https://www2.census.gov/prod2/popscan/p60-049.pdf.

NOTES

4. "Public Improvement Program for Laurinburg, North Carolina," North Carolina Digital Collections, 1960, https://digital.ncdcr.gov/documents/detail/2310550?item=2342806.

5. "Public Improvement Program for Laurinburg, North Carolina."

6. "Public Improvement Program for Laurinburg, North Carolina."

7. Richard Rothstein, *The Color of Law: A Forgotten History of How Our Government Segregated America* (Liveright, 2017), 223.

8. City of Laurinburg, Neighborhood Analysis, Laurinburg, North Carolina, 1967.

9. David L. Lewis, *W.E.B. Du Bois: A Biography* (Henry Holt and Company, 2009).

10. "Scotland County's Integration Story Told," *Laurinburg Exchange*, August 21, 2015, https://www.laurinburgexchange.com/news/1603/scotland-countys-integration-story-told.

11. Scott Witten, "Laurinburg Native Would Like to Restore Historic Hotel," *Laurinburg Exchange*, November 20, 2015, www.laurinburgexchange.com/news/23211/scotland-county-native-has-grand-plans-for-downtown-site.

12. Shomari Wills, *Black Fortunes: The Story of the First Six African Americans Who Escaped Slavery and Became Millionaires* (Amistad, 2018), 2–5.

13. Arpita Aneja and Olivia B. Waxman, "Beyond Tulsa: The Historic Legacies and Overlooked Stories of America's 'Black Wall Streets,'" *Time*, May 29, 2021, https://time.com/6050811/tulsa-black-wall-street/.

14. "What Is an Echo Chamber?," GFC Global, May 29, 2021, https://edu.gcfglobal.org/en/digital-media-literacy/what-is-an-echo-chamber/1/.

15. "What Is an Echo Chamber?"

Postscript: The Spirit Prevails

1. "About Booker T. Washington," Techie Homes, accessed May 12, 2025, https://techie-homes.com/ceo.

2. Don Morfe, "Original Richmond Cotton Mill," The Historical Marker Database, September 21, 2014, https://www.hmdb.org/m.asp?m=77351.

NOTES

3. Albert Muzquiz, "Black America's Hard-Fought Integration of Southern Textile Mills," Heddels, June 24, 2020, https://www.heddels.com/2020/06/segregation-in-southern-textile-mills/.

4. "NCORR Grants Scotland County $9.6 Million for Affordable Housing," *Laurinburg Exchange*, November 2, 2023, https://www.laurinburgexchange.com/news/breaking-news/261696/ncorr-grants-scotland-county-9-6-million-for-affordable-housing.

About the Authors

LAURETTA MALLOY NOBLE and LEEANÉT NOBLE are critically acclaimed internationally for breaking boundaries and boxes, and empowering and inspiring others through creative mediums. They have been performing and working together creatively for the past thirty years. Their work in fashion with Rick Owens has been featured in major publications such as *Vogue*, *Elle*, *The Wall Street Journal*, *The Washington Post*, *The New York Times*, and *Ebony*, and in museums worldwide , including the Design Museum in London, the Museum of Modern Art, and the Brooklyn Museum.

As performing artists and creatives, both individually and as a duo, they have worked with or opened for Rihanna, Alicia Keys, Disney Theatrical Productions, *Stomp*, Lauryn Hill, Chaka Khan, and Earth, Wind & Fire, among others.

As a writing duo, their play *Lerato and Her Drum* was a finalist in the TYA ReImagine: New Plays competition, and they have penned articles for Arianna Huffington's Thrive Global platform as well as DC Theater Arts celebrating Black history. Both attended Howard University's newly named Chadwick A. Boseman College of Fine Arts and collectively have certifications in genealogy, organizational behavior, filmmaking, and script writing. Their production company, the Loncie Project, Inc., celebrates culture and the arts through riveting collaborations with fashion houses and brands, live productions, film, music, and free lessons and workshops for young artists with financial needs around the world. Their band, Loncie's Living Room, blends soul, jazz, and contemporary music and can be heard in the WHUT-PBS program *Black Stage: Classical Canon*.

Through their writing, live productions, films, scripts, and work with major brands, Lauretta and LeeAnét seek to enlighten, engage, and entertain in unique, groundbreaking ways.